T0220574

Beginning Machine Learning in iOS

CoreML Framework

Mohit Thakkar

Apress®

Beginning Machine Learning in iOS: CoreML Framework

Mohit Thakkar
Vadodara, Gujarat, India

ISBN-13 (pbk): 978-1-4842-4296-4　　　　ISBN-13 (electronic): 978-1-4842-4297-1
https://doi.org/10.1007/978-1-4842-4297-1

Library of Congress Control Number: 2019932985

Managing Director, Apress Media LLC: Welmoed Spahr
Acquisitions Editor: Natalie Pao
Development Editor: James Markham
Coordinating Editor: Jessica Vakili

Cover designed by eStudioCalamar

Cover image designed by Freepik (www.freepik.com)

Distributed to the book trade worldwide by Springer Science+Business Media New York, 233 Spring Street, 6th Floor, New York, NY 10013. Phone 1-800-SPRINGER, fax (201) 348-4505, e-mail orders-ny@springer-sbm.com, or visit www.springeronline.com. Apress Media, LLC is a California LLC and the sole member (owner) is Springer Science + Business Media Finance Inc (SSBM Finance Inc). SSBM Finance Inc is a **Delaware** corporation.

For information on translations, please e-mail rights@apress.com, or visit www.apress.com/rights-permissions.

Apress titles may be purchased in bulk for academic, corporate, or promotional use. eBook versions and licenses are also available for most titles. For more information, reference our Print and eBook Bulk Sales web page at www.apress.com/bulk-sales.

Any source code or other supplementary material referenced by the author in this book is available to readers on GitHub via the book's product page, located at www.apress.com/978-1-4842-4296-4. For more detailed information, please visit www.apress.com/source-code.

Printed on acid-free paper

In loving memory of Steven Paul Jobs (1955 to 2011) - the man who was crazy enough to change the world.

Dedicated to all the tech enthusiasts out there trying to make a dent in the universe. It is you guys who make this world a better place for the people inhabiting it.

Cheers to you!

Love,

Mohit

Table of Contents

About the Author

Mohit Thakkar is an Associate Software Engineer with MNC. He has a bachelor's degree in computer engineering and is the author of several independently published titles, including *Artificial Intelligence, Data Mining & Business Intelligence, iOS Programming,* and *Mobile Computing & Wireless Communication.* He has also published a research paper titled "Remote Health Monitoring using Implantable Probes to Prevent Untimely Death of Animals" in the International Journal of Advanced Research in Management, Architecture, Technology and Engineering.

About the Technical Reviewer

Felipe Laso is a Senior Systems Engineer working at Lextech Global Services. He's also an aspiring game designer/programmer. You can follow him on Twitter as @iFeliLM or on his blog.

Acknowledgments

I'd like to take this opportunity to gratefully thank the people who have contributed toward the development of this book:

Aaron Black, Senior Editor at Apress, and James Markham, Development Editor at Apress who saw potential in the idea behind the book. They helped kick-start the book with their intuitive suggestions and made sure that the content quality of the book remains uncompromised.

Felipe Laso, Technical Reviewer of the book who made sure that the practical aspects of the book are up to the mark. His insightful comments have been of great help in refinement of the book.

Jessica Vakili, Coordinating Editor at Apress who made sure that the process from penning to publishing the book remained smooth and hassle free.

Mom, dad, and my sweet little sister, all of whom were nothing but supportive about the entire idea of writing a book. They have always been there for me, encouraging me to achieve my aspirations.

Countless number of mentors and friends who have guided me at every little step of life.

You who wish to refine your skills by reading this book so that you can make a difference in the lives of those around you. You encourage me to contribute toward collaborative education.

Thanks!

CHAPTER 1

Introduction to Machine Learning

This chapter provides a basic explanation of the concept of machine learning (ML) along with information about its applications, types of ML, how it works, and why we need it. Even if you are a novice to the concept, this chapter should help you with the information you need to get started with ML. It is a fun chapter, with lots of pictures and examples to help you understand the text.

What Is Machine Learning?

In the past few years, ML, also referred to as automated learning, has been one of the fastest growing areas in the field of computer science and information technology. As the term suggests, machine learning is a process during which a machine learns about significant patterns in a given set of input data. Now you might be wondering what the word "pattern" means in this context. Consider Figure 1-1 to get a clearer idea.

© Mohit Thakkar 2019
M. Thakkar, *Beginning Machine Learning in iOS*,
https://doi.org/10.1007/978-1-4842-4297-1_1

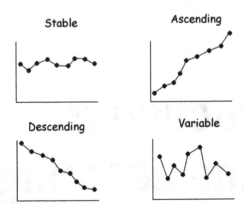

Figure 1-1. *Data patterns*

This figure demonstrates a mapping of four sets of data points on their corresponding graphs. As we do that, the data points in the data set form a unique pattern. The patterns observed in the figure are Stable, Ascending, Descending, and Variable. Learning about such data patterns can be used to develop an algorithm that helps the machine to adapt and react appropriately when it encounters alien data. The goal of ML is to make a machine react automatically to alien data based on the learning. For instance, if the machine observes that the given data set forms a stable pattern where data points deviate from -1 to +1, it can predict the value of the next data point that will be added to the data set.

To sum it up, ML is the process of creating programs that learn from data and make predictions. Some of the well-known ML models are as follows:

- *Ensemble learning*: Combination of several ML algorithms (classifiers) to obtain a better predictive performance as compared with any one ML algorithm alone. Figure 1-2 shows the flow of control in ensemble learning.

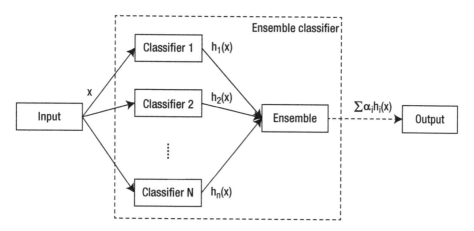

Figure 1-2. *Ensemble learning*

- *Support vector machine (SVM)*: It is a classifier that is
  formally defined by a separating hyperplane. Given
  some labeled training data, the SVM algorithm outputs
  an optimal hyperplane that categorizes new examples.
  In two-dimensional space, this hyperplane is a line
  dividing a plane in two parts. Consider Figure 1-3 to get
  a better idea.

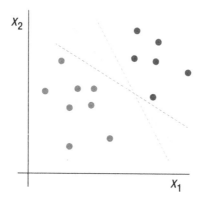

Figure 1-3. *Support vector machine*

- *Artificial neural network (ANN)*: It is an interconnected network of nodes that is designed to process information in the same way as a human brain does it. The information is stored in an ANN in the form of interconnections between nodes. It takes in the input, processes the input based on the stored information, and generates the output. Figure 1-4 shows the interconnections between nodes in an ANN.

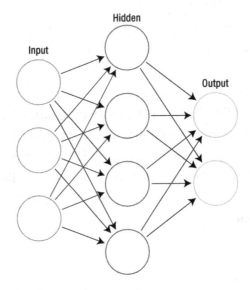

Figure 1-4. *Artificial neural network*

- *Decision tree*: It uses a tree-like graph that predicts the item's target value based on observations about the item. Figure 1-5 demonstrates a decision tree that helps you make the decision of accepting or rejecting a job offer.

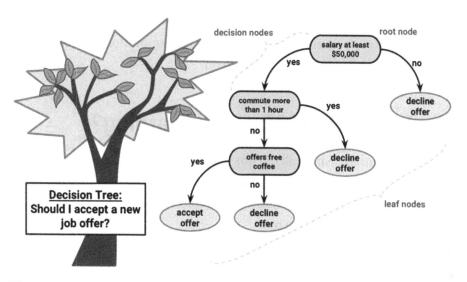

Figure 1-5. Decision tree

What Are the Applications of Machine Learning?

ML is a tool that we knowingly or unknowingly use in many of our day to day activities. Following are some of the familiar ML applications:

- An e-mail service filters spam e-mail.

- A digital camera detects human faces.

- Personal digital assistants (PDAs) detect voice commands.

- Optical character recognition (OCR) software recognizes characters from an image.

- Online payment gateways detect credit card fraud.

- Websites display personalized advertisements to a user.

Apart from the aforementioned applications, ML is also used in various other domains such as medical diagnosis, space exploration, wildlife preservation, sentiment analysis, and so on.

Why Do We Need Machine Learning?

Let's say we want to display all the images of roses in our application from the user's photo library. This seems like a simple task, so we can do some programming. Perhaps, we'll start with the color. If the dominant color in the picture is red, maybe it's a rose.

```
// Use Color
If color == "reddish"
```

Figure 1-6 shows different types of roses. Looking at the figure, you will notice that there are many roses that are white or yellow in color. So, we'll go forward and start describing the shape. And soon we'll realize that it's very difficult to write even such a simple program programmatically. Hence, this is where we turn to ML for our help. Rather than describing how a rose looks programmatically, we will describe a rose empirically.

Figure 1-6. *Different types of roses*

ML has two steps. In the first step, you collect images of roses, lilies, sunflowers, and other flowers and label them. You will run them through a learning algorithm and you will get what we call a model. This model is an empirical representation of what a rose looks like. This step is known as learning. In the second step, you do the following:

- Take a picture of a rose.

- Embed the model generated in step one in your app.

- Run the picture of a rose through the model.

You will get a label for the picture and the confidence level. See Figure 1-7. This step is known as inference.

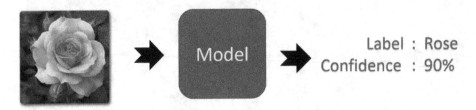

Figure 1-7. *Inference*

This is how we harness the potential of ML to simplify our tasks.

How Does Machine Learning Work?

In layman terms, ML can be thought of as converting past experiences into expertise. Let us consider the task of recognizing spam e-mails and labelling them. To perform this task, the machine will create a set of all the e-mails that were previously labeled as spam e-mails by a human user; the machine will then identify all the terms whose appearance in the e-mail is an indication of spam e-mail. Now when a new e-mail appears, the machine scans it for suspicious words identified from the set of previous spam e-mails to identify if the new e-mail is a spam. This way, the machine will be able to label new e-mails correctly and automatically.

Let us consider another task that involves ML, that is, the detection of human faces by camera application. This functionality helps the camera to make sure that all the faces are in focus before the picture gets captured. See Figure 1-8. To automatically detect a human face, the camera needs to know the structure of a human face. For this purpose, a learning algorithm is applied in the camera application, during which it works with a training data set consisting of a variety of human faces. By analyzing all the human faces in the training data set, the camera observes the common pattern in all the data members of the training data set. For instance, it may observe that all the human faces consist of two eyes, one nose, and a pair of lips. Along with that it might also observe the positioning of these elements. By learning this, the camera will now be able to detect human faces automatically.

Figure 1-8. *Facial recognition*

There are many algorithms that are used for ML. One such algorithm is the Perceptron Learning Algorithm. The following section discusses this algorithm to get a clearer idea about ML.

Perceptron Learning Algorithm

The Perceptron is a classic example of a neural network that gives a binary output based on the input it receives. We can use a Perceptron for a classification task where we need to classify the input in one of two output categories. For instance, consider Figure 1-9, which presents a linearly separable problem. Here, the goal is to create a Perceptron that separates red dots from blue dots. To do this, the Perceptron must first analyze the training data set and determine a straight line on the graph that separates the blue dots from the red ones. Once that is done, the Perceptron will be able to classify new input vectors as blue dots or red dots by determining their position on the graph in relation to the line.

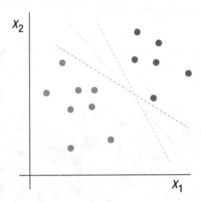

Figure 1-9. *Linearly separable problem*

Following is the learning process for the Perceptron to determine the line that separates the two categories of input vectors:

- The goal is to obtain a straight line based on the training data set that separates the red dots from the blue dots. So, let us consider the equation of a straight line:

$$ax + by + c = 0$$

$$x = -\frac{c}{a} - \frac{b}{a} y$$

- We now get an equation of the straight line. The position of the line completely depends on the values of a, b, and c. So, we can adjust the value of weights (a, b and c) as per our requirements.

- Now, initialize the weights (a, b and c) to random real values.

- Iterate through the training data set, collecting all data members misclassified by the current set of weights. If all the data members are classified correctly, substitute the values of the weights in the equation of the line. You've found the line that separates the red dots from the blue ones.

- Or else, modify the weights (a, b and c) depending on the misclassified data members and iterate again through the training data set. Repeat the process until all the data members are classified correctly.

Types of Machine Learning

There are broadly three types of ML algorithms:

1. *Supervised learning*: This type of learning algorithm consists of a training data set that has pairs consisting of input values and desired output values. Such data is known as labeled training data. In such algorithms, a mapping function is generated that maps the input values in the training data set to their corresponding output values. Supervised learning represents the concept of humans teaching the computer. It is mainly used to perform classification tasks.

2. *Unsupervised learning*: This type of learning algorithm consists of a training data set that has only input values, no output values. Such data is

known as unlabeled training data. In such learning algorithms, learning occurs purely based on the structure of the data. Unsupervised learning represents the concept of computers teaching themselves. It is mainly used to solve clustering tasks.

3. *Reinforcement learning*: This type of learning algorithm interacts with the environment by producing actions and discovering error or success. This type of learning allows machines to automatically determine the ideal behavior within a specific environment. Simple feedback is required for the machine to learn which action is best; this is known as the reinforcement signal.

Now that you are aware of the basics of ML, we will discuss the core ML framework provided by Apple to implement pretrained ML models into iOS applications.

Summary

- Machine Learning is a process during which a machine learns about significant patterns in a given set of data so that it can make predictions.

- Ensemble learning, SVMs, ANNs, and decision trees are some of the well-known ML models.

- Spam e-mail filtering, face detection, voice recognition, OCR, credit card fraud detection, and personalized advertisements are common examples of ML.

- Advanced applications of ML include medical diagnosis, space exploration, wildlife preservation, and sentiment analysis.

- ML identifies patterns in historical data and uses this knowledge to react appropriately to any alien data that it might encounter in the future.

- Perceptron is a classic example of ML that gives a binary output based on the input it receives. It can be used to solve a linearly separable problem.

- ML algorithms are broadly classified into three types: supervised, unsupervised, and reinforcement learning.

Introduction to Core ML Framework

In Chapter 1, you learned the basic definition of machine learning (ML), how it works, where it is used, and what is required to use it. This chapter will introduce you to the Core ML framework that was introduced by Apple Inc. in 2017 to allow application developers to implement ML in their iOS applications. You will also learn the concepts of training and inference, which will give you a clearer picture of how ML works.

This chapter also provides a step-by-step guide for creating an ML application for an iOS device. You need not to worry if you have not created an iOS application previously, because this chapter will guide you through the entire process of creating an application from scratch.

Core ML at a Glance

Core ML is a groundbreaking application development framework released by Apple. It allows you to use pretrained ML models in your iOS applications.

Traditionally, ML applications had to rely on cloud services to run third-party ML algorithms. This caused the application to run very slow on mobile devices. But with the launch of Core ML, ML applications can now locally run optimized and trained ML algorithms on the device, leading to faster processing speed (Figure 2-1).

© Mohit Thakkar 2019
M. Thakkar, *Beginning Machine Learning in iOS*,
https://doi.org/10.1007/978-1-4842-4297-1_2

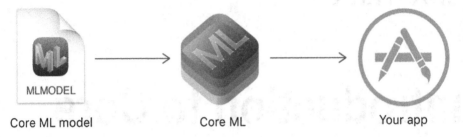

Figure 2-1. *Core ML applications lead to faster processing time*

Core ML is huge, and it can be used to implement a multitude of functionalities. However, there are two direct applications of Core ML:

- First, the developers can use the pretrained models that already exist in the Core ML.

- Second, they can they can build their own custom ML model using frameworks like Caffe, Turi, and Keras, and then convert it into a Core ML model to use it in their iOS application.

Some well-known applications that use the functionality provided by Core ML are Pinterest (image-based search), iPhone Photo Library (groups photos together), and Nude App (recognizes pictures with nudity).

Figure 2-2 shows the process of converting an ML model created using third-party frameworks into the Core ML format so that you can use it in your application.

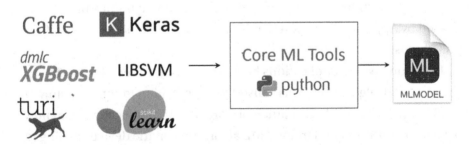

Figure 2-2. *Converting to Core ML*

Core ML offers support for a wide range of ML algorithms such as ensemble learning, support vector machines (SVMs), artificial neural networks (ANNs), linear models, and so on. However, Core ML will only run models that are trained with labeled data. It does not provide support for unsupervised models.

Core ML Components

Core ML is Apple's ML framework available for macOS, iOS, watchOS, and tvOS. It acts as a foundation for Apple's previous ML frameworks—Accelerate and Metal Performance Shaders (MPS)—which are commonly used as performance primitives. Accelerate uses CPUs for memory-heavy tasks, while MPS uses GPU for compute-heavy tasks. Core ML decides which underlying framework to use based on the requirement of the application. Figure 2-3 shows various components of the Core Ml framework. In addition to Accelerate and MPS, Core ML provides support for the following domain-specific frameworks:

- *Vision*: Vision is Apple's one-stop shop to do all the things related to computer vision and images. It is a framework that is comprised of computer vision algorithms that help in performing tasks such as detection and classification of images and videos. It can be used to do things like object tracking or deep learning-based face detection.

- *Natural Language*: This is Apple's one-stop shop to do text processing. It is a framework that can be used to analyze natural language and deduce some metadata from it. It is helpful for performing tasks like named entity recognition (NER), text prediction, language identification, and sentiment analysis.

- *GameplayKit*: It is a framework that helps to incorporate common gameplay behavior such as pseudorandom number generation, object motion, and path finding in your application. It is an object-oriented framework that contains reusable components that help you build games.

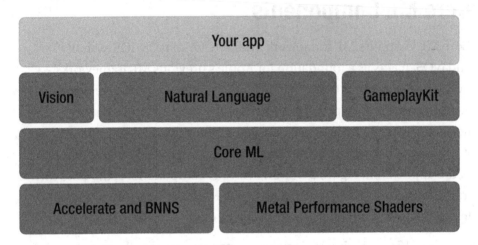

Figure 2-3. *Core ML components*

You can think of Core ML as a set of tools that helps you in bringing multiple ML models together and wrap them in one interface so that you can easily use them in your application code.

Training and Inference

In Chapter 1 you learned that ML is a process of discovering patterns in a given data set to make predictions. To do so, we need the following entities:

- *Input data points*: Let's say we want to classify a student as Pass/Fail. In this case, the input data points will be comprised of the marks of various students.

- *Expected outputs for the given input points*: Continuing our previous example of classification, the expected outputs would consist of Pass or Fail.

- *A learning algorithm*: This is the algorithm that learns how to map input to the output and create rules that can be used to deal with new inputs (inference). These rules are created by the process called training.

Let us consider some examples to understand this more clearly.

Example 1 (image recognition): A model that is learning to identify strollers on a street is trained with millions of images of streets. These images are known as a training data set. Some of the images contain no pedestrians at all, while others have up to 50. Multiple learning algorithms are trained on the data (street images), with each having access to the correct answers. Each algorithm develops a variety of models to identify strollers on streets. This process is known as training. After this, when a new image is fed as an input to the algorithm, it will apply the appropriate model and determine the number of strollers in the image. This process is known as inference.

Example 2 (sorting): A model is learning to sort items using visual identification. It picks out recyclable items from the lot as it passes on a conveyor belt. It places items such as glass, plastic, paper, and metal into their respective bins. This process is known as inference. Each item is labeled with an identification number. Once a day, human experts examine the bins and inform the robot about the items that were incorrectly sorted. The robot uses this feedback to improve. This process is known as training.

Example 3 (decision making): A model is learning to make an estimate of risk associated with financial investment. The model is fed a large amount of data on the transactions that investors made in the past, along with the outcomes of those transactions. Based on this training data, the model calculates the risk-to-reward ratio. This is known as training. Now, when the model is fed with certain parameters about an investment, it can predict the risk associated with that investment. This is known as inference.

Machine Learning Models

A model, in terms of machine learning, is nothing but a function that takes in some input and returns some output. It is generated by the process of training and inference, that is, applying a training data set to a learning algorithm. The learning algorithm finds patterns in training data that maps the input data points in the data set to their corresponding output data points. The algorithm then returns an ML model that captures these data patterns.

Most of the models that you might want to use in your application have some key function at their core. Some of the usual functionalities offered by ML models (see Figure 2-4) are sentiment analysis, handwriting recognition, language translation, image classification, style transfer, music tagging, and text prediction.

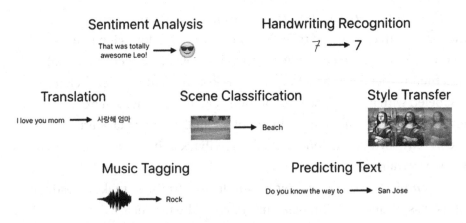

Figure 2-4. *Key functionalities of ML models*

Core ML supports a variety of models, including neural networks, tree ensembles, support vector machines, and linear models. It requires the ML models to be in Core ML format, that is, files with a .mlmodel file extension. Apple provides several open source ML models that are already built in the Core ML framework. However, you can create your own custom ML model, convert it into Core ML format, and use it in your application.

In the following part of this chapter, we will learn how to create a simple iOS application, and implement an open source ML model in that application.

Beginning with Xcode

Tightly integrated with the Core ML framework, Xcode is an incredibly productive IDE (integrated development environment) by Apple that's used to build applications for MacBook, iPhone, iPad, Apple Watch, and Apple TV.

Following are the configurations that we'll be using as a general development practice for this chapter:

- *Xcode*: version 9.4.1 or later

- *Deploy SDK*: version 11.4 or later

- *Programming language*: Swift 4 or later

- *Simulator*: iPhone 8 Plus or later

Assuming that you are familiar with the Mac environment and you have Xcode installed on your MacBook, let us begin building our first iOS application.

Step 1: Launch Xcode. It should display a welcome dialog (Figure 2-5). From here, choose "Create a new Xcode project" to start a new project.

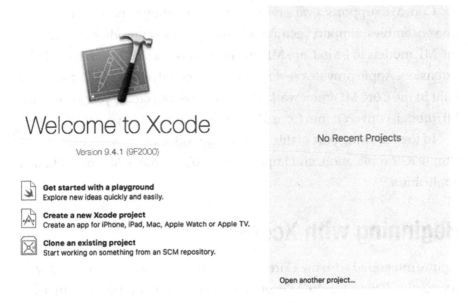

Figure 2-5. *Xcode welcome dialog*

Step 2: Xcode shows you various devices and project templates for your application (Figure 2-6). Choose your target device and appropriate template (Single View App). Then click "Next."

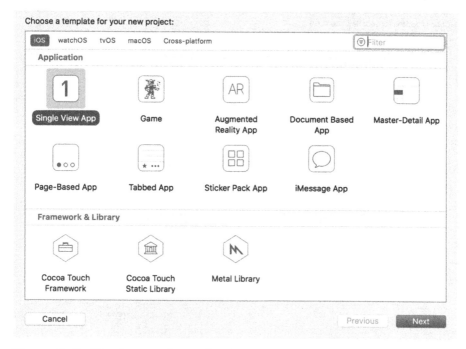

Figure 2-6. *Xcode template selection*

Step 3: This brings you to another screen to fill in all the necessary options for your project (Figure 2-7). The options include the following:

- *Product Name*: The name of your application.

- *Organization Name*: You can fill in this box with your company's name.

- *Organization Identifier*: This is the domain name written in reverse order. If you have a domain, you can use your own domain name.

- *Class Prefix*: Xcode uses the class prefix to name the class automatically. You can choose your own prefix or leave it blank.

- *Devices*: Select the device on which you want your application to run.

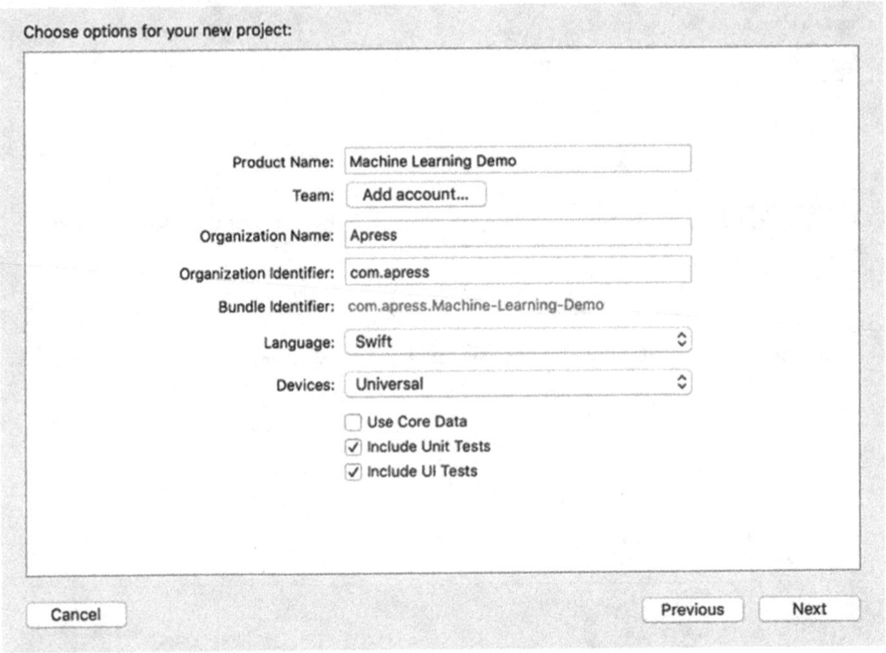

Choose options for your new project:

Product Name: Machine Learning Demo

Team: Add account...

Organization Name: Apress

Organization Identifier: com.apress

Bundle Identifier: com.apress.Machine-Learning-Demo

Language: Swift

Devices: Universal

☐ Use Core Data
☑ Include Unit Tests
☑ Include UI Tests

Cancel   Previous   Next

Figure 2-7. *Xcode project options*

Step 4: Xcode then asks you where you want to save your project
(Figure 2-8). Pick any folder (e.g., Desktop) on your Mac and click "Create."

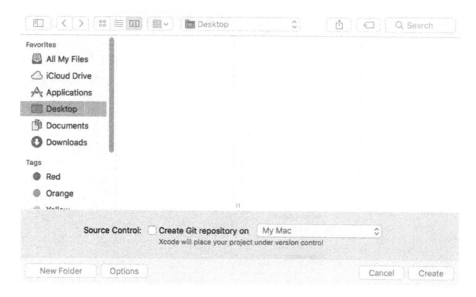

Figure 2-8. *Xcode folder picker*

Step 5: As you confirm, Xcode automatically creates your project based on all the options you provided. The next screen will look similar to Figure 2-9.

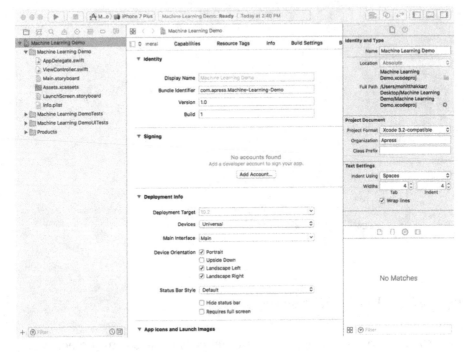

Figure 2-9. *Xcode main window*

Before moving on to the code segment, let us familiarize ourselves with the Xcode workspace (Figure 2-10).

- On the left pane, it's the project navigator. You can find all your files under this area.

- The center part of the workspace is the editor area.

- The rightmost pane is the utility area. This area displays the properties of the file and allows you to access Quick Help.

- There's a toolbar at the top that provides various functions for you to run your app, switch editor, and so on.

Toolbar

Editor Area

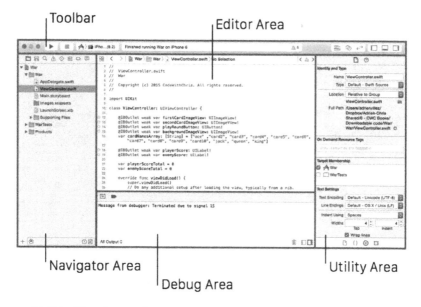

Navigator Area

Debug Area

Utility Area

Figure 2-10. *Xcode workspace*

Step 6: In the project navigator area, you will find a file that goes by the name 'MainStoryboard.storyboard'. Select this file and you will notice that the editor area changes to an interface builder (Figure 2-11) that shows an empty screen for your application.

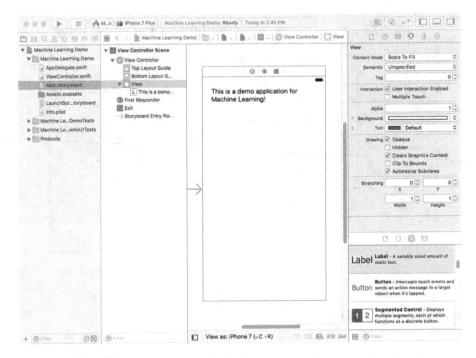

Figure 2-11. *Xcode interface builder*

Step 7: In the lower part of the utility area, you'll find the object library. From here, you can choose any of the UI controls and drag-and-drop it into the view. Let us pick "Label" and drag it into the view. You can change the text of the label from the object attributes in the utility area. You can also add positioning constraints as per your requirements for proper structuring of the UI elements.

Step 8: Now it's time to test your app. You can run it using the run icon on the toolbar. Xcode automatically builds the app and runs it in the simulator. If everything is fine, your app should run properly in the simulator.

That's it! We just created our first iOS application. In the following section we'll learn to integrate an open-source ML model in this application.

Photos Application Using Xcode

Let us now create an application that allows the user to select an image from the photo library and displays the selected image on the screen. We will later modify this application to include an ML model in it.

Step 1: Launch Xcode and open the application "Machine Learning Demo" that we created previously.

Step 2: Open the interface builder by opening the file that goes by the name "MainStoryboard.storyboard" from the navigator area.

Step 3: Delete the label that we created previously. Now, add a Button followed by an Image View to the interface by dragging the controls from the object library in the utility area to the interface builder. See Figure 2-12 for reference. You can change the color and text of the button from the object attributes in the utility area.

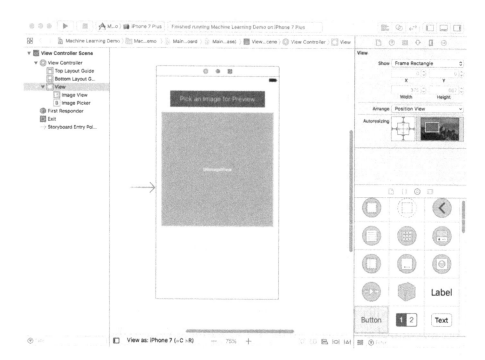

Figure 2-12. *Photos application interface*

Step 4: Now that we've created the interface, we'll focus on the logic of our application. Open the assistant editor by clicking its icon on the right end of the toolbar. Load the file called "ViewController.swift" in the assistant editor. You'll simultaneously see the interface builder on the left part of the window and your code ("ViewController.swift") on the right part of the window. See Figure 2-13 for reference.

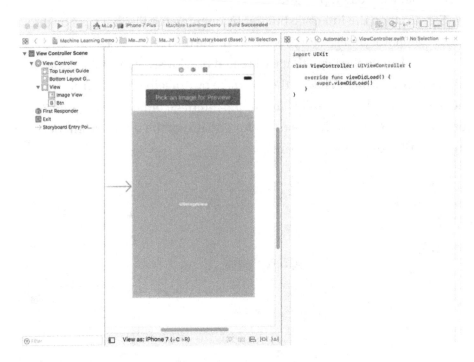

Figure 2-13. *Assistant editor*

Step 5: To connect interface elements to the code, we need to create outlets and actions. Outlets are used to modify properties of the UI elements, while the actions are used to handle events related to the UI elements. We will create outlets for Button and Image View. In order to do so, control and drag from the Button/Image View to the code ("ViewController.swift") and create an IBOutlet. In the connection field, we will choose Outlet; as Name we will use btn or imageView; and as Type we will select UIButton or UIImageView. That should create the following IBOutlet code in your ViewController class:

```
@IBOutlet weak var btn: UIButton!
@IBOutlet weak var imageView: UIImageView!
```

Step 6: At the tap of the button, the app should open an image picker that allows the user to select an image from the photo library and return the selected image. Let us now create an action that will handle the click event for the button. To do so, again control and drag from the button to the code. You should see a popup similar to Figure 2-14. In the connection field we will choose Action; as Name we will use pickImageBtnClick; the Event that fires the action is "Touch Up Inside"; and the argument passed to the method is Sender.

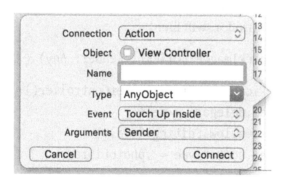

Figure 2-14. *IBAction*

That should create the following IBAction code in your ViewController class:

```
@IBAction func pickImageBtnClick(_ sender: Any) {

    //code
}
```

Step 7: Now let us add the code that will handle the button click. First of all, since we need the user to interact with the photo library, we have to conform to the UIImagePickerControllerDelegate protocol as well as UINavigationControllerDelegate protocol. Add both controllers to your class definition in the ViewControllor.swift file:

```
class ViewController: UIViewController,
UIImagePickerControllerDelegate, UINavigationControllerDelegate {

    //code
}
```

Step 8: When the user clicks the button, we need to create an instance of UIImagePickerController and set its delegate to our current class. We also need to specify the source for the image picker as the photo library. Once the picker is created, we need to present it modally using the present method. To do so, add the following code to the pickImageBtnClick method in ViewControllor.swift file:

```
@IBAction func pickImageBtnClick(_ sender: Any) {

    let imagePicker = UIImagePickerController()
    imagePicker.delegate = self
    imagePicker.allowsEditing = false
    imagePicker.sourceType = .photoLibrary

    present(imagePicker, animated: true, completion: nil)
}
```

Step 9: Since we are confirming to UIImagePickerControllerDelegate, we need to implement two delegate methods: imagePickerController and imagePickerControllerDidCancel. The imagePickerController method is called when the user is finished selecting the image from the library. Hence, we will use this method to set the selected image in the Image View of our application. The imagePickerControllerDidCancel method is called when the user cancels the image picker. Hence, in this method, we will simply dismiss the picker. Add the following code to the ViewController class in the ViewControllor.swift file:

```
func imagePickerController(_ picker: UIImagePickerController,
didFinishPickingMediaWithInfo info: [String : Any]) {

    let pickedImage = info[UIImagePickerControllerOriginal
    Image] as! UIImage

    imageView.image = pickedImage
    self.dismiss(animated: true, completion: nil)
}

func imagePickerControllerDidCancel(_ picker: UIImagePicker
Controller) {

    self.dismiss(animated: true, completion: nil)
}
```

Note that if you are using Swift 4.2, the preceding code might not work for you, since it is written in Swift 4.0. Following is the code that you will use instead:

```
func imagePickerController(_ picker: UIImagePickerController,
didFinishPickingMediaWithInfo info: [UIImagePickerController.
InfoKey : Any]) {

    let pickedImage = info[UIImagePickerController.InfoKey.
    originalIm    age] as! UIImage

    imageView.image = pickedImage
    picker.dismiss(animated: true)
}
```

```
func imagePickerControllerDidCancel(_ picker:
UIImagePickerController) {

    self.dismiss(animated: true, completion: nil)
}
```

If everything is alright, your final swift code (Swift 4.0) should be as follows:

```
import UIKit

class ViewController: UIViewController,
UIImagePickerControllerDelegate, UINavigationControllerDelegate
{

    @IBOutlet var btn: UIButton!
    @IBOutlet var imageView: UIImageView!

    override func viewDidLoad() {
        super.viewDidLoad()
        btn.layer.cornerRadius = 8
    }

    @IBAction func pickImageBtnClick(_ sender: Any) {
        let imagePicker = UIImagePickerController()
        imagePicker.delegate = self
        imagePicker.allowsEditing = false
        imagePicker.sourceType = .photoLibrary

        present(imagePicker, animated: true, completion: nil)
    }

    //UIImagePickerControllerDelegate Methods

    func imagePickerController(_ picker: UIImagePickerController,
    didFinishPickingMediaWithInfo info: [String : Any]) {
```

```
    let pickedImage = info[UIImagePickerController
    OriginalImage] as! UIImage

    imageView.image = pickedImage
    self.dismiss(animated: true, completion: nil)
}

func imagePickerControllerDidCancel(_ picker: UIImagePicker
Controller) {
    self.dismiss(animated: true, completion: nil)
}
}
```

Step 10: Since our application needs to access the photo library of the user's device, we need to ask the user to grant access for the same. Otherwise, our application might terminate unexpectedly. To avoid that, we need to add the following property in the "Info.plist" file (Figure 2-15) of our application:

- *Key*: Privacy – Photo Library Usage Description

- *Value*: $(PRODUCT_NAME) photo use

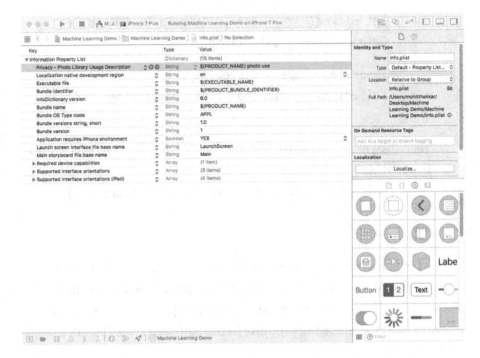

Figure 2-15. *Information property list*

That's it! We just created an iPhone application that allows the user to pick an image from the photo library and displays the selected image on the screen. It's time to test our application. You can run the application using the run icon on the toolbar. Xcode automatically builds the app and runs it in the simulator (Figure 2-16). If everything is fine, your app should run properly in the simulator.

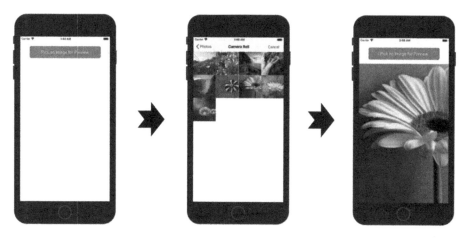

Figure 2-16. *Photos application using Xcode*

Using a Core ML Model in Your Application

The most wonderful part about Core ML is that it lets you integrate pretrained models in your application. And this can be done even if you do not have an extensive knowledge about neural networks or ML. The only constraint is that the model should be in Core ML format to integrate it in your application. In this part of the book, we will use a model that is already in Core ML format and is available on Apple's website.

The application that we built in the previous section of this chapter lets the user select a picture from their device's photo library. We will now integrate a Core ML model in this application, which will try to predict the label for the object in the selected picture. To do so, we will need to first download the model. Go to Apple's Developer website on ML (https://developer.apple.com/machine-learning/build-run-models/) and scroll to the bottom of the page. You will see a section listing all the pretrained Core ML models that are available to download for free (Figure 2-17).

Places205-GoogLeNet

Detects the scene of an image from 205 categories such as an airport terminal, bedroom, forest, coast, and more.

View original model details ›

Download Core ML Model ⊕

ResNet50

Detects the dominant objects present in an image from a set of 1000 categories such as trees, animals, food, vehicles, people, and more.

View original model details ›

Download Core ML Model ⊕

Inception v3

Detects the dominant objects present in an image from a set of 1000 categories such as trees, animals, food, vehicles, people, and more.

View original model details ›

Download Core ML Model ⊕

Figure 2-17. *Apple Core ML models*

The model that we will be using for our application is Inceptionv3. This model is originally built using Keras and is converted to Core ML format using Python tools. It detects presiding objects in an image from more than 1,000 categories such as trees, animals, food, vehicles, people, flowers, and so on. Please feel free to use any other model from the list instead of Inceptionv3, as the process is almost similar for all the Core ML Models. Let us see a step-by-step procedure to integrate this model in our application.

Step 1: First, we will need to add a label to the application interface to display the prediction for the selected image. To do so, go to the interface builder and decrease the height of the imageView to make space for the label at the bottom. Now drag and drop a label from the object library into the interface. See Figure 2-18 for reference.

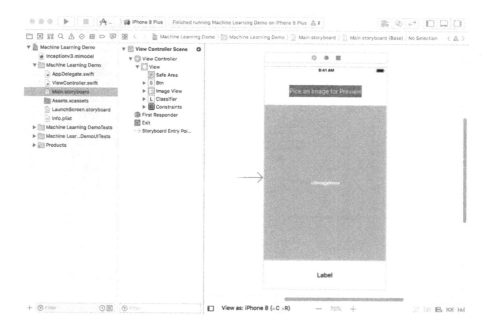

Figure 2-18. *Photos application updated interface*

Step 2: Add an outlet for the newly created label so that we can change its text later.

```
@IBOutlet weak var classifier: UILabel!
```

Step 3: Now that we have prepared the interface for the prediction, let us put the model to work. You will have the Inceptionv3.mlmodel file that you downloaded from the Apple website previously. Drag and drop that file under your project folder in the Xcode project navigator. This will add the Core ML model in your application.

Step 4: Select the model file from the navigator and you will notice that the Xcode automatically recognizes the file as an ML model. It displays information about the model such as type of the model (which in our case is Neural Network Classifier), the author details, model description, and so on (Figure 2-19).

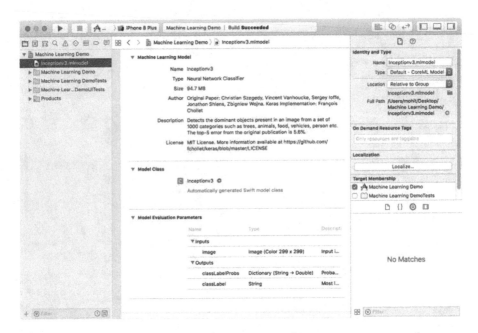

Figure 2-19. *Core ML model (Inceptionv3)*

It also displays the Model Class, which is automatically generated from the ML model and can be directly used in our application. Click the arrow next to the class name and you will be able to see the implementation code of the model class.

Other important information that the Xcode displays is the Model Evaluation Parameters. This is the information about the input that the model takes in and the output that it returns. In our case, the model takes in a colored image of size 299×299 as an input and it returns a string as output.

Step 5: Now let us use the model class in our application to make predictions. Go to the ViewController.swift file and import the Core ML framework in the very beginning.

```
import CoreML
```

Step 6: Declare a model variable in the ViewController class that will represent the Core ML model.

```
var model:Inceptionv3!
```

Step 7: Override the viewWillAppear() method of the ViewController class and initialize the model in that method.

```
override func viewWillAppear(_ animated: Bool) {
    model = Inceptionv3()
}
```

Step 8: The input that our model takes in is an image of size 299×299. Thus, we will need to resize the image after the user is done selecting the image. We will write the code for this in the delegate method imagePickerController(). The following code will do the job for us:

Note   The numbering in the following lines of code is just added for the explanation that follows.

```
//resize image
```

1. UIGraphicsBeginImageContextWithOptions (CGSize(width: 299, height: 299), true, 2.0)
2. pickedImage.draw(in: CGRect(x: 0, y: 0, width: 299, height: 299))
3. let newImage = UIGraphicsGetImageFromCurrentImageContext()!
4. UIGraphicsEndImageContext()

CHAPTER 2   INTRODUCTION TO CORE ML FRAMEWORK

```
5. let attrs = [kCVPixelBufferCGImageCompatibilityKey:
   kCFBooleanTrue, kCVPixelBufferCGBitmapContextCompatibilityKey:
   kCFBooleanTrue] as CFDictionary
6. var pixelBuffer : CVPixelBuffer?
7. let status = CVPixelBufferCreate(kCFAllocatorDefault,
   Int(newImage.size.width), Int(newImage.size.height),
   kCVPixelFormatType_32ARGB, attrs, &pixelBuffer)

8. guard (status == kCVReturnSuccess) else {
9. return
10. }

11. CVPixelBufferLockBaseAddress(pixelBuffer!, CVPixelBuffer
    LockFlags(rawValue: 0))
12. let pixelData = CVPixelBufferGetBaseAddress(pixelBuffer!)

13. let rgbColorSpace = CGColorSpaceCreateDeviceRGB()
14. let context = CGContext(data: pixelData, width:
    Int(newImage.size.width), height: Int(newImage.size.
    height), bitsPerComponent: 8, bytesPerRow: CVPixelBuff
    erGetBytesPerRow(pixelBuffer!), space: rgbColorSpace,
    bitmapInfo: CGImageAlphaInfo.noneSkipFirst.rawValue)

15. context?.translateBy(x: 0, y: newImage.size.height)
16. context?.scaleBy(x: 1.0, y: -1.0)

17. UIGraphicsPushContext(context!)
18. newImage.draw(in: CGRect(x: 0, y: 0, width: newImage.
    size.width, height: newImage.size.height))
19. UIGraphicsPopContext()
20. CVPixelBufferUnlockBaseAddress(pixelBuffer!, CVPixelBuff
    erLockFlags(rawValue: 0))
```

Now, let us understand what is happening in the preceding code. Since our model accepts an input image of size 299×299, lines 1-4 convert the selected image to that size and assign it to a new variable called newImage.

It is important to know that the model accepts an input image in form of pixels. Hence, lines 5-10 store the newImage in the form of a pixel buffer, which basically holds the image in the form of pixels in the memory. This buffer will be supplied as an input for prediction.

Then, all the pixels present in the image are converted into device-dependent RGB color space. Lines 11-13 do that. In line 14, we store the pixel data in CGContext so that we can easily modify some properties of the image pixels. We then scale the image as per our requirement in lines 15-16. Lines 17-20 update the final image buffer.

Note that it's okay if you do not understand most parts of this code. The only thing you need to know is that we took the picture that the user selected from the photo library and converted it into a form that the model accepts for prediction.

Step 9: Finally, it's time to call the prediction method of the model that will do the image prediction for us. Add the following code in the delegate method imagePickerController() right after the image resizing code.

```
//predict image label

guard let prediction = try? model.prediction(image:
pixelBuffer!) else {

        classifier.text = "Can't Predict!"
        return
}

classifier.text = "This is probably \(prediction.classLabel)."
```

The prediction method is supplied with the pixel buffer as a parameter. If the prediction is successful, the method returns an object that gives us the output label. We set this output label text to the classifier label that we added to the interface earlier. If the prediction is not successful, we manually set the classifier label text to let the user know that the model was unable to predict the label for the selected image.

Step 10: It is finally time to build and run the application. Let us find out how well our first ML application does. Figures 2-20 to Figure 2-24 show different screens that you should see while playing around with your application.

Figure 2-20. *Photos application prediction (A)*

Figure 2-21. *Photos application prediction (B)*

Figure 2-22. *Photos application prediction (C)*

Figure 2-23. *Photos application prediction (D)*

Figure 2-24. *Photos application prediction (E)*

Summary

- Core ML is a framework by Apple that can be used to develop machine learning applications for Apple products such as iPhone, iPad, MacBook, Apple TV, and Apple Watch.

- Core ML allows developers to use pretrained ML models, which are already in Core ML format, to implement ML functionalities in their applications.

- Core ML also allows developers to convert custom ML models into Core ML format to use it their applications.

- Core ML integrates the model within the application package so that the ML algorithms can run locally instead of remotely. This results in faster processing speeds.

- Core ML is based on Apple's previous frameworks— Accelerate and Metal Performance Shaders (MPS)— that act as performance primitives.

- The major components of Core ML are:

  - *Vision*: Classification of images and videos

  - *Natural Language*: Text-based prediction and sentiment analysis

  - *GameplayKit*: Implements gameplay behavior

- An ML model can be trained using input data points, output for each input data point, and a learning algorithm that maps the input data points to their corresponding output. Once trained, a model can be used for inference.

- The usual functionalities offered by ML models are sentiment analysis, handwriting recognition, language translation, image classification, text prediction, and so on.

CHAPTER 3

Custom Core ML Models Using Turi Create

In Chapter 2, you learned how to use pretrained machine learning models in your application. In this chapter, you will learn how to train your own model with a third-party framework using Turi Create. You will also find a step-by-step guide on how to convert this trained model into the Core ML format and use it in your application.

Necessity for a Custom Model

An ML model can be thought of as a piece of code that we use to add intelligent user experiences in our application. As we learned in Chapter 2, an ML model can be used to perform a variety of tasks; and just like any other piece of code, there is no single model that can be used to carry out all the intelligent tasks. For instance, consider the following tasks that you might want to implement in your application:

- Ability to take a picture of your food and know how many calories you are consuming

- Changing the presentation slides on a TV screen with a simple gesture on your iPhone

© Mohit Thakkar 2019
M. Thakkar, *Beginning Machine Learning in iOS*,
https://doi.org/10.1007/978-1-4842-4297-1_3

- Tracking an object in real time

- Trying out artistic filters on photographs

- Categorizing the music files as per their genres

This is just a small list; there are an endless number of intelligent tasks that you might want your application to perform. All these tasks demonstrate very different user experiences; hence there is no single ML model that can accommodate all of these tasks. This is where the need for a custom model arises. All these tasks have some things in common—the fact that they all use ML and they all require very little data to implement them in our application. Hence, we can create a custom ML model for each of the tasks that we want to perform.

Life Cycle of a Custom Model Creation

In order to create a custom Core ML model, the first thing you will need to do is to identify the problem you are trying to solve and collect data that will help you solve the problem. For instance, if you are trying to create a model that will predict your next month's electricity bill, the data you will need to collect are your historical electricity bills and your electricity consumption statistics for the corresponding time period.

Once you have the dataset, the next step is to train the model using an appropriate algorithm. Once the training is done, you can check the accuracy by evaluating the model. Finally, if you are satisfied with the evaluation results, you can build the model. If not satisfied, you can pass the model through another iteration of the training process. You can repeat the process for as long as you are unsatisfied with the results. Figure 3-1 shows the life cycle of custom model creation.

Note   Apple has introduced a standardized file format called ML Model (.mlmodel) that allows developers to use machine learning in their application. All the machine learning models need to be eventually converted into the Core ML format (.mlmodel) in order to use them in Apple products.

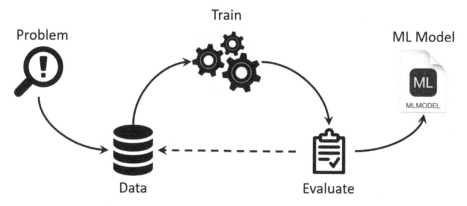

Figure 3-1. *Life cycle of custom model creation*

Following are the steps involved in creation of a custom Core ML model:

1. *Problem*: The first step of custom model creation involves identifying the problem that we are trying to solve and understanding it in terms of ML. Consider the tasks in Table 3-1 and their corresponding ML category.

Table 3-1. *Machine Learning Tasks*

Task You Want to Do	Machine Learning Terminology
Label images	Image Classification
Recognize objects within images	Object Detection
Find similar images	Image Similarity
Create custom styled avatars	Style Transfer
Personalize user choices	Recommender
Detect activity using sensors	Activity Classification
Analyze sentiment from message	Text Classifier
Predict a label	Classifier
Predict a numeric value	Regression
Group similar data together	Clustering

2. *Data*: Once we identify the problem, the next step is to identify the type of data and the amount of data that we will need to accomplish this task. For supervised learning, the data will consist of pairs of input and the corresponding output. Data can be in any form such as pictures, text files, CSV files, or tables. Finally, we collect relevant data that we will use to train our model.

3. *Train*: Once we've collected the required data, we can start training our model on the data.

4. *Evaluate*: Once the model is ready, we can determine its quality by evaluating the model's success ratio against a test dataset. If the results are not up to the mark and the model is not ready for production, we can reiterate the training process until the model becomes more accurate.

5. *Model*: If the results of the training process are satisfactory, we can generate the .mlmodel that can be used in our applications.

Training and evaluating a model from scratch can be a complicated task. To simplify this complexity, Apple has introduced Turi Create. Using Turi Create in collaboration with Python will allow us to train our custom model based on existing ML models using very few lines of code, but more on that later.

Assembling Data

Before learning about assembling data, let us understand the basic types of tasks that we can accomplish using ML. If you have lots of images, you might be interested in categorizing those images on the basis of their content; if your application shows advertisement to the users, you might want to customize those advertisements as per the user preference; or you might want to prompt users about the duplicate contacts in their phonebook.

All these tasks require different types of data. For understanding, let us consider the following problem statement that we will try to solve:

Problem   Given a picture of a dog, the application should be able to predict the breed of the dog.

To create a model that can do this task, we will need lots of images of dogs from different breeds. We will then create a dataset from these images. Don't worry; it's not as complicated as it sounds. First, create a folder called Dataset on your MacBook. Inside the Dataset folder, create subfolders for each breed of dog you want to classify. Then inside each subfolder, place some images of dogs of that breed. Note that the name of the subfolder should be the name of the dog breed. Refer to Figure 3-2 for reference.

Figure 3-2. *Dataset for custom ML model*

That's it. We now have the dataset required to train our model to perform the classification task. In the following section of this chapter, we will learn how to train an ML model using the dataset.

Introduction to Turi Create

Turi Create is a Python-based framework that helps you create Core ML models directly from the dataset. It is an open-source framework available at https://github.com/apple/turicreate. It is also cross-platform, which means that you can use it on both MacOS and Linux.

The major benefit of using Turi Create is that rather than training a model from scratch, it allows us to train our model on the top of the ML model that already exists in the OS. This is commonly known as transfer learning. This is important because training a model from scratch requires millions of images, huge computing power, and lots of patience. Instead, using Turi Create, we can use existing ML models such as ResNet (residual networks) and train the last few layers of this model to our specific data. This way we can create a sufficiently good ML model using the amount of data that we have and in time. Using transfer learning also results in smaller model size.

Note   We will be using Mac OS Mojave 10.14 and Xcode 10 for all the development that we do here onward.

Let us learn how to install Turi Create on our Mac.

Step 1: To install Turi Create, we will need Python installed on our Mac. By default, we have Python 2.7 installed on Mac systems. This would be sufficient for installing Turi Create. You can manually download Python from https://www.python.org and install it on your Mac if you wish to. But note that Turi Create does not support the latest version of Python (i.e., version 3.7); hence we will use the default version of Python that is installed on our systems. To check the Python version on your system, you can open the terminal window and run the "python" command. See Figure 3-3.

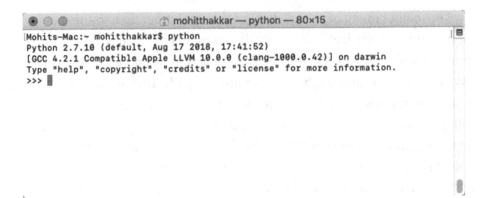

Figure 3-3. *Checking Python version on Mac*

Step 2: Now, in order to install packages using Python, you need to install the Python package manager (commonly known as pip) on your system. To do so, open the terminal window and run the "sudo easy_install pip" command. See Figure 3-4. Sit back and wait while the package manager gets installed on your system.

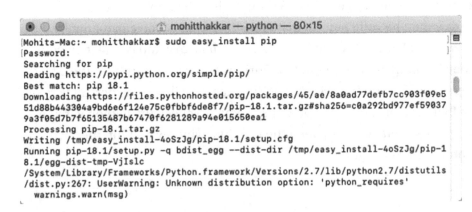

Figure 3-4. *Installing pip on Mac*

Step 3: Open the terminal window again and run the "pip" command to check if the Python package manager is successfully installed on your system. If it is installed, then you will see a list of commands offered by the package manager (Figure 3-5). If not, please try reinstalling pip on your Mac before proceeding to the next step.

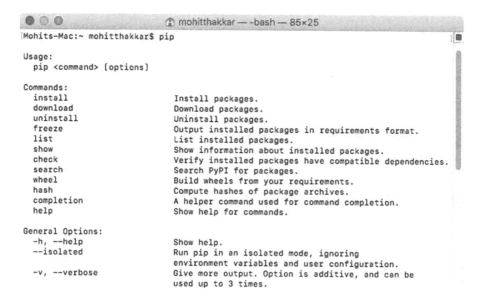

Figure 3-5. Python commands

Step 4: Now that pip is successfully installed on your Mac, you can use it to install Turi Create. Open the terminal window and run the following command to install the latest version of Turi Create on your machine (see Figure 3-6 for the output):

```
pip install turicreate
```

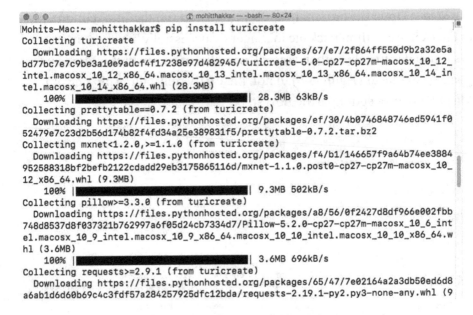

Figure 3-6. *Installing Turi Create*

You have now successfully installed Turi Create on your machine. In the following section, we will learn how to use it to create a custom ML model.

Training and Evaluating a Custom Model

Following are the steps to create a custom ML model using Turi Create:

Step 1: Open Xcode; select **File ➤ New ➤ File** in the menu (Figure 3-7).

Figure 3-7. *New file in Xcode*

Step 2: Select Blank file from template selection menu (Figure 3-8).

Figure 3-8. *Xcode template selection*

Step 3: Name the file **MyCustomModel.py**

Step 4: Save it to desktop.

Step 5: Import Turi Create by adding the following line of code:

```
import turicreate as tc
```

Step 6: Define the path for the training dataset by adding the following code:

```
url = "dataset/"
```

Step 7: Add the following code to search and load images from the dataset folder:

```
data = tc.load_images(url)
```

Step 8: Now we will define the image category and save it in the **"dogBreed"** property. We will fetch the folder name from the path of the image to determine the image category. To do so, add the following code:

```
data["dogBreed"] = data["path"].apply(lambda path: path.
split('/')[1])
```

This will create a labeled dataset where each image in our training dataset will have a path and a property called **"dogBreed"**.

Step 9: Now, we will save the new labeled dataset as an SFrame. This SFrame will be used to train the data. Add the following code to save the dataset as an SFrame:

```
data.save("dogBreed.sframe")
```

Step 10: Let us preview the new labeled data on Turi Create. To do so, add the following code:

```
data.explore()
```

Step 11: To load the SFrame for training purposes, write the following code:

```
dataBuffer = tc.SFrame("dogBreed.sframe")
```

Step 12: Now we will train the model using 90% of the data and test the model using the remaining 10% of the data. To do so, write the following code:

```
trainingBuffers, testingBuffers = dataBuffer.random_split(0.9)

model = tc.image_classifier.create(trainingBuffers,
target="dogBreed", model="squeezenet_v1.1")
```

Here, we are training our model on top of the **"Squeezenet"** model that already exists. You can use other models like **"ResNet-50"** for more accuracy.

Step 13: It is now time to evaluate the test data to determine the accuracy of the model. To do so, add the following code:

```
evaluations = model.evaluate(testingBuffers)
print evaluations["accuracy"]
```

Step 14: Finally, add the following code to save the model and export it to the Core ML format:

```
model.save("dogBreed.model")
model.export_CoreML("dogBreed.mlmodel")
```

Your final code for MyCustomModel.py should be as in Figure 3-9.

```
1  import turicreate as tc
2
3  #load images
4  url = "dataset/"
5  data = tc.load_images(url)
6  data["dogBreed"] = data["path"].apply(lambda path: path.split('/')[1])
7  data.save("dogBreed.sframe")
8  data.explore()
9
10 #train model
11 dataBuffer = tc.SFrame("dogBreed.sframe")
12 trainingBuffers, testingBuffers = dataBuffer.random_split(0.9)
13 model = tc.image_classifier.create(trainingBuffers, target="dogBreed",
       model="squeezenet_v1.1")
14
15 #evaluate model
16 evaluations = model.evaluate(testingBuffers)
17 print evaluations["accuracy"]
18
19 #save model
20 model.save("dogBreed.model")
21 model.export_coreml("dogBreed.mlmodel")
22 |
```

Figure 3-9. *MyCustomModel Python code*

To execute this code, open the Terminal app on your Mac and change the current directory to the location of your Python file. Then execute the code using the following command:

```
python MyCustomModel.py
```

It might take several minutes while the Python code is executing. First, the code will load the images from the dataset into the memory, then the images will be labeled based on the folder they reside in, and then they will be converted to an SFrame that will be used for training. Note that you do not need to explicitly do anything; the process will automatically start once you have executed the Python code in the terminal window. All you need to do is sit back and wait for the code to give you a Core ML model. The terminal screen in Figure 3-10 shows the process.

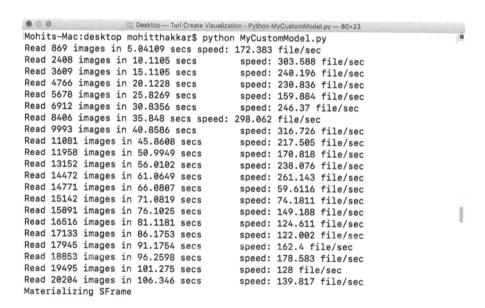

Figure 3-10. *Loading images and creating an SFrame*

Now, the explore() method that we used in step 10, to preview the labeled images, will open the Turi Create Visualization window (see Figure 3-11) that will preview the images.

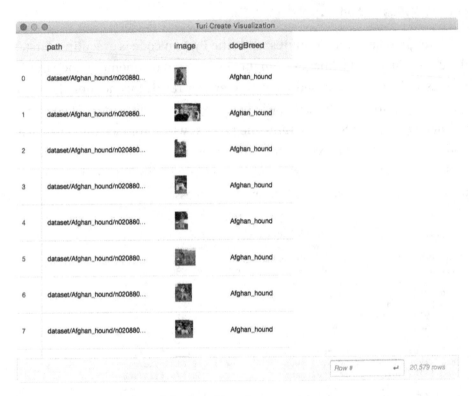

Figure 3-11. *Turi Create Visualization*

You can see the labeled training data here. Meanwhile, the code will continue executing in the terminal window. The code will now load the SFrame that we created previously, download the base ML model (Squeezenet in this case), and start training the SFrame on the top of the base model. The terminal screen in Figure 3-12 shows the process.

```
● ○ ○                    Desktop — Turi Create Visualization - Python MyCustomModel.py — 90×28
Materializing SFrame
Downloading base mlmodel
Downloading https://docs-assets.developer.apple.com/coreml/models/SqueezeNet.mlmodel to /v
ar/folders/y5/qksq72c51w39y89dwv0s48100000gn/T/model_cache/squeezenet_v1.1.mlmodel
Analyzing and extracting image features.
+---------------------+-----------------+--------------------+
| Images Processed    | Elapsed Time    | Percent Complete   |
+---------------------+-----------------+--------------------+
| 64                  | 2.27s           | 0.25%              |
| 192                 | 4.55s           | 1%                 |
| 256                 | 4.67s           | 1.25%              |
| 320                 | 6.73s           | 1.5%               |
| 640                 | 12.74s          | 3.25%              |
| 960                 | 20.39s          | 5%                 |
| 1280                | 27.20s          | 6.75%              |
| 1600                | 37.28s          | 8.5%               |
| 1920                | 43.21s          | 10.25%             |
| 2240                | 53.18s          | 12%                |
| 2560                | 1m 0s           | 13.75%             |
| 2880                | 1m 7s           | 15.5%              |
| 3200                | 1m 13s          | 17.25%             |
| 3520                | 1m 19s          | 19%                |
| 3840                | 1m 25s          | 20.75%             |
| 4160                | 1m 31s          | 22.25%             |
| 4480                | 1m 39s          | 24%                |
| 4800                | 1m 45s          | 25.75%             |
| 5120                | 1m 56s          | 27.5%              |
| 5440                | 2m 4s           | 29.25%             |
```

Figure 3-12.   *Training the dataset*

After the training process, the code will evaluate the model to see if it
is accurate enough. This evaluation will be done on the testing data that
we randomly picked from the dataset. This random pick will be done as a
result of the one-line code we wrote for (0.9, 0.1) split on the dataset, for
using 90% of the dataset for training and 10% of the dataset for testing.
There will be multiple iterations for the evaluation process, and the code
will also print the accuracy for each iteration. The terminal screen in
Figure 3-13 shows the process.

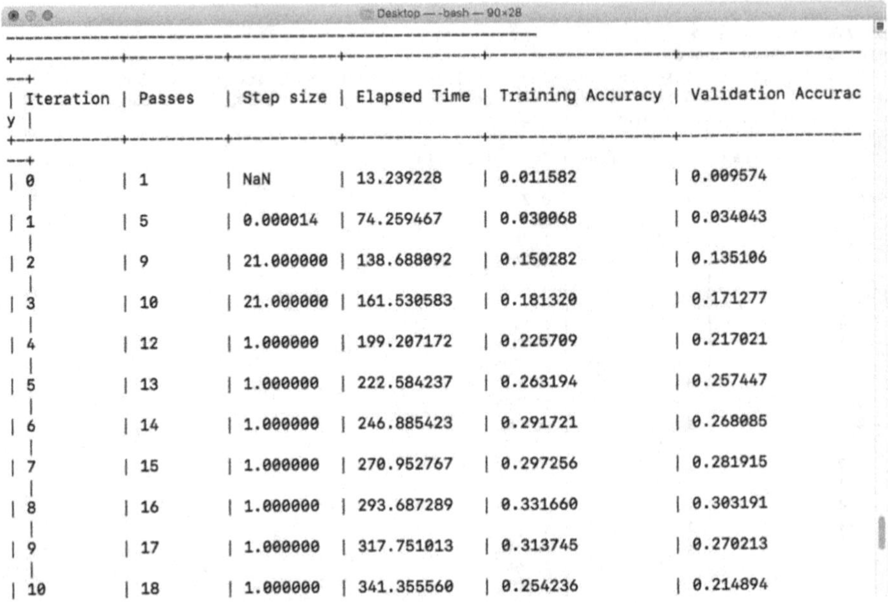
Desktop — -bash — 90×28
| Iteration | Passes | Step size | Elapsed Time | Training Accuracy | Validation Accurac
y |
0	1	NaN	13.239228	0.011582	0.009574
1	5	0.000014	74.259467	0.030068	0.034043
2	9	21.000000	138.688092	0.150282	0.135106
3	10	21.000000	161.530583	0.181320	0.171277
4	12	1.000000	199.207172	0.225709	0.217021
5	13	1.000000	222.584237	0.263194	0.257447
6	14	1.000000	246.885423	0.291721	0.268085
7	15	1.000000	270.952767	0.297256	0.281915
8	16	1.000000	293.687289	0.331660	0.303191
9	17	1.000000	317.751013	0.313745	0.270213
10	18	1.000000	341.355560	0.254236	0.214894

Figure 3-13. *Evaluating the model*

Once the evaluation is done, the code will save the model and convert it to the Core ML format. You will see some new items generated on your Mac (Figure 3-14).

Figure 3-14. *Custom model files*

That's it. You just created a Core ML model using Turi Create. This model can now be used in your iOS applications to classify the breed of a dog, given its picture.

Converting a Custom Model into Core ML

If you are using Turi Create to generate a model from scratch, you do not need to worry about conversion because it already creates a model in the Core ML format; but if you are using other tools like Caffe, TensorFlow, or Keras, you might be wondering how to convert models built using those tools to the Core ML format. To do that, Apple has introduced Core ML Tools alongside Core ML. It is an open-source Python package that takes ML models in a variety of formats and converts them into the Core ML format.

Let us learn how to use Core ML Tools to convert models into the Core ML format. To do so, you will need Python installed on your machine. If you do not have it, please install the recent version of Python from https://www.python.org. We will take a Caffe model and convert it into the Core ML format. To do so, consider the following steps:

Step 1: Open the Terminal application on your Mac and install Core ML Tools using the Python package manager. To do so, type in the following command:

```
pip install CoreMLtools
```

Step 2: Open Xcode; select **File ➤ New ➤ File** in the menu (Figure 3-15).

Figure 3-15. *New file in Xcode*

Step 3: Select Blank file from template selection menu (Figure 3-16).

Figure 3-16. *Xcode template selection*

Step 4: Name the file **MyConverter.py**

Step 5: Save it to desktop.

Step 6: Download the Caffe model that you want to convert to the Core ML format. Note that when you download a Caffe model, you will have three different files:

- **modelName.caffemodel** – The model file

- **deploy.prototxt** – The file that contains the network structure

- **labels.txt** – The file that contains the output values for the prediction

Step 7: Open the MyConverter.py file and add the following code to import Core MLtools:

```
import CoreMLtools
```

Step 8: Our Caffe model is defined by two files: ".caffemodel" and ".prototxt". So, let us add it into the code by adding the following lines of code:

```
caffe_model = ('oxford102.caffemodel', 'deploy.prototxt')
```

Step 9: Next, we will define our class labels file by adding the following code:

```
labels = 'class_labels.txt'
```

Step 10: Now to convert the Caffe model into the Core ML format, add the following line of code:

```
CoreML_model = Core MLtools.converters.caffe.convert
(caffe_model, class_labels = labels)
```

Step 11: Finally, we can save the converted model by adding the following code to our file:

```
CoreML_model.save('MyCustomModel.mlmodel')
```

Your final code should be as in Figure 3-17.

```
1  import coremltools
2
3  caffe_model = ('oxford102.caffemodel', 'deploy.prototxt')
4  labels = 'class_labels.txt'
5
6  coreml_model =
       coremltools.converters.caffe.convert(caffe_model,
       class_labels = labels)
7
8  coreml_model.save('MyCustomModel.mlmodel')|
9
```

Figure 3-17. *Converting from Caffe to Core ML (code)*

Step 12: To execute the code, open the Terminal app on your Mac, change the current directory to the location of your Python file, and type the following command (see Figure 3-18 for output).

```
python MyConverter.py
```

```
● ● ○                          ▨ oxford102 — -bash — 99×32
Mohits-Mac:oxford102 mohitthakkar$ python MyConverter.py

================ Starting Conversion from Caffe to CoreML =======================
Layer 0: Type: 'Input', Name: 'input'. Output(s): 'data'.
Ignoring batch size and retaining only the trailing 3 dimensions for conversion.
Layer 1: Type: 'Convolution', Name: 'conv1'. Input(s): 'data'. Output(s): 'conv1'.
Layer 2: Type: 'ReLU', Name: 'relu1'. Input(s): 'conv1'. Output(s): 'conv1'.
Layer 3: Type: 'Pooling', Name: 'pool1'. Input(s): 'conv1'. Output(s): 'pool1'.
Layer 4: Type: 'LRN', Name: 'norm1'. Input(s): 'pool1'. Output(s): 'norm1'.
Layer 5: Type: 'Convolution', Name: 'conv2'. Input(s): 'norm1'. Output(s): 'conv2'.
Layer 6: Type: 'ReLU', Name: 'relu2'. Input(s): 'conv2'. Output(s): 'conv2'.
Layer 7: Type: 'Pooling', Name: 'pool2'. Input(s): 'conv2'. Output(s): 'pool2'.
Layer 8: Type: 'LRN', Name: 'norm2'. Input(s): 'pool2'. Output(s): 'norm2'.
Layer 9: Type: 'Convolution', Name: 'conv3'. Input(s): 'norm2'. Output(s): 'conv3'.
Layer 10: Type: 'ReLU', Name: 'relu3'. Input(s): 'conv3'. Output(s): 'conv3'.
Layer 11: Type: 'Convolution', Name: 'conv4'. Input(s): 'conv3'. Output(s): 'conv4'.
Layer 12: Type: 'ReLU', Name: 'relu4'. Input(s): 'conv4'. Output(s): 'conv4'.
Layer 13: Type: 'Convolution', Name: 'conv5'. Input(s): 'conv4'. Output(s): 'conv5'.
Layer 14: Type: 'ReLU', Name: 'relu5'. Input(s): 'conv5'. Output(s): 'conv5'.
Layer 15: Type: 'Pooling', Name: 'pool5'. Input(s): 'conv5'. Output(s): 'pool5'.
Layer 16: Type: 'InnerProduct', Name: 'fc6'. Input(s): 'pool5'. Output(s): 'fc6'.
Layer 17: Type: 'ReLU', Name: 'relu6'. Input(s): 'fc6'. Output(s): 'fc6'.
Layer 18: Type: 'Dropout', Name: 'drop6'. Input(s): 'fc6'. Output(s): 'fc6'.
WARNING: Skipping training related layer 'drop6' of type 'Dropout'.
Layer 19: Type: 'InnerProduct', Name: 'fc7'. Input(s): 'fc6'. Output(s): 'fc7'.
Layer 20: Type: 'ReLU', Name: 'relu7'. Input(s): 'fc7'. Output(s): 'fc7'.
Layer 21: Type: 'Dropout', Name: 'drop7'. Input(s): 'fc7'. Output(s): 'fc7'.
WARNING: Skipping training related layer 'drop7' of type 'Dropout'.
Layer 22: Type: 'InnerProduct', Name: 'fc8_oxford_102'. Input(s): 'fc7'. Output(s): 'fc8_oxford_102
'.
Layer 23: Type: 'Softmax', Name: 'prob'. Input(s): 'fc8_oxford_102'. Output(s): 'prob'.
```

Figure 3-18. *Converting from Caffe to Core ML (execution)*

When the code execution is finished, you will see the output model file (Figure 3-19) in the Core ML format.

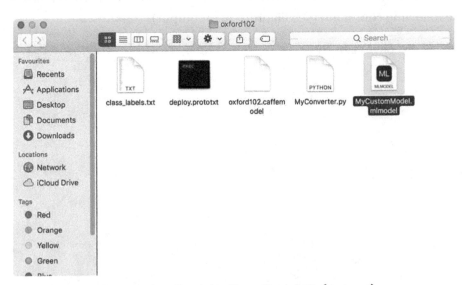

Figure 3-19. *Converting from Caffe to Core ML (output)*

That's the process for converting a Caffe model into the Core ML format using Core ML Tools.

Using a Custom Model in Your Application

Once a model is created or converted to the Core ML format, you can use it in your applications in the same way as you would use one of the Apple-provided Core ML models. Let us use in our application the model that we created using Turi Create to predict the breed of the dog, given its image. For this, we will create an application using Xcode 10 that will allow users to pick an image of a dog from the photo library of their device. The application will then display the image along with the breed of the dog that is displayed in the image. Follow these steps:

Step 1: Launch Xcode 10. It should display a welcome dialog. From here, choose "Create a new Xcode project" to start a new project (Figure 3-20).

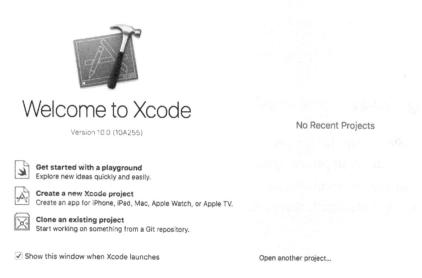

Welcome to Xcode
Version 10.0 (10A255)

No Recent Projects

> **Get started with a playground**
> Explore new ideas quickly and easily.

> **Create a new Xcode project**
> Create an app for iPhone, iPad, Mac, Apple Watch, or Apple TV.

> **Clone an existing project**
> Start working on something from a Git repository.

☑ Show this window when Xcode launches

Open another project...

Figure 3-20. *Welcome to Xcode*

Step 2: Xcode shows you various devices and project templates for your application (Figure 3-21). Choose your target device and appropriate template (Single View Application). Then click "Next."

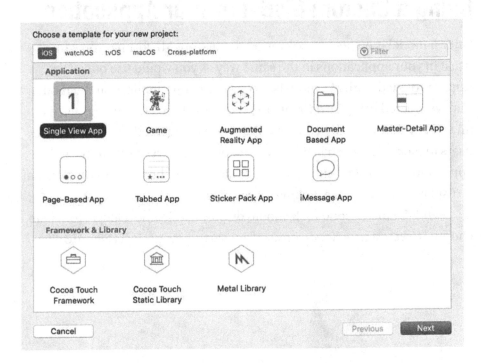

Figure 3-21. *Xcode template selection*

Step 3: This brings you to another screen to fill in all the necessary options for your project (Figure 3-22). The options include Product Name, Organization Name, Organization Identifier, Class Prefix, Devices , and so on. Fill in the details and go to the next step.

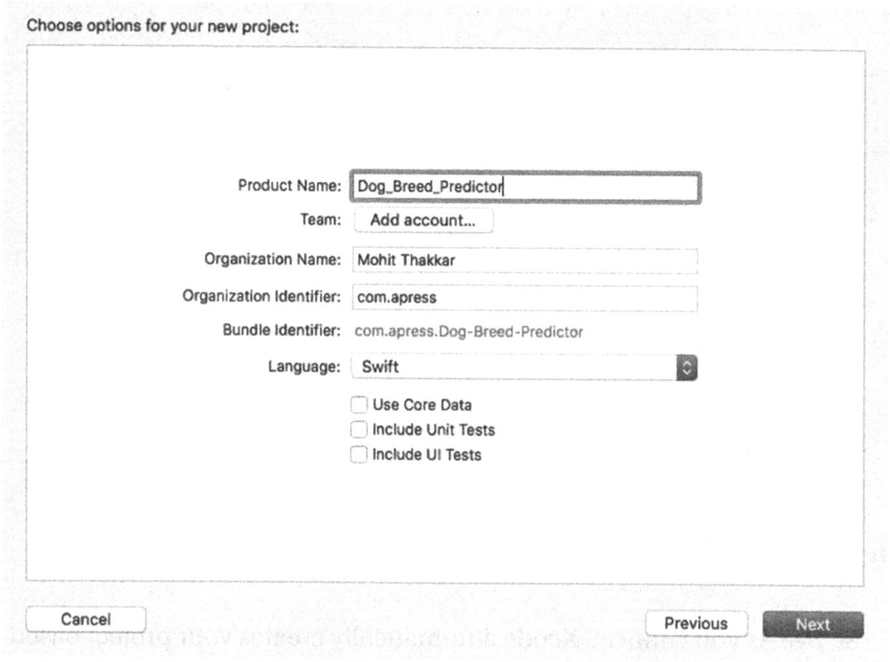

Choose options for your new project:

Product Name:	Dog_Breed_Predictor
Team:	Add account...
Organization Name:	Mohit Thakkar
Organization Identifier:	com.apress
Bundle Identifier:	com.apress.Dog-Breed-Predictor
Language:	Swift

☐ Use Core Data
☐ Include Unit Tests
☐ Include UI Tests

Cancel   Previous   Next

Figure 3-22. Xcode project options

Step 4: Xcode then asks you where you want to save your project (Figure 3-23). Pick any folder (e.g., Desktop) on your Mac and click "Create."

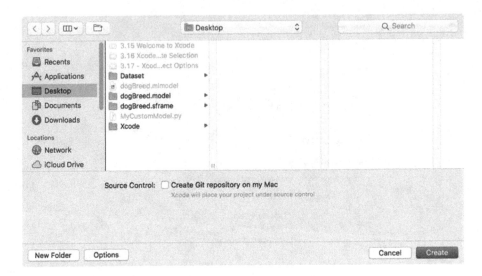

Figure 3-23. *Xcode folder picker*

Step 5: As you confirm, Xcode automatically creates your project based on all the options you provided. From the navigator pane, select the **"Main.storyboard"** file to open the interface builder for your application. See Figure 3-24 for reference.

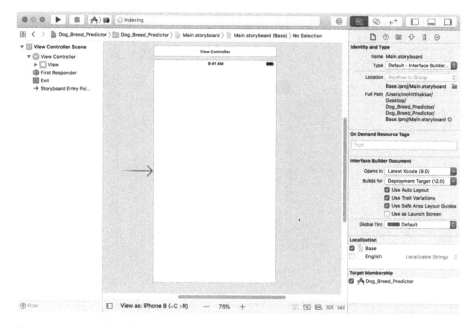

Figure 3-24. *Xcode interface builder*

Step 6: Add a Button followed by an Image View to the interface by dragging the controls from the object library in the utility area to the interface builder. You can change the color and text of the button from the object attributes in the utility area. Also add a label to the application interface to display the prediction for the selected image. See Figure 3-25 for reference.

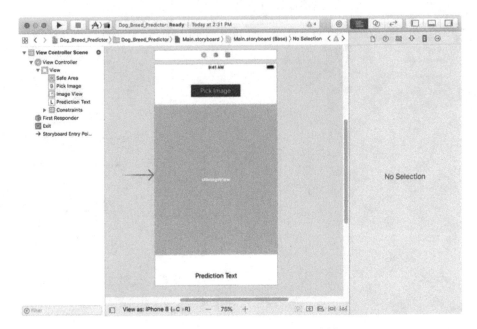

Figure 3-25. *Dog breed predictor application interface*

Step 7: Open the assistant editor by clicking its icon on the right end of the toolbar. Load the file called **"ViewController.swift"** in the assistant editor. You'll simultaneously see the interface builder on the left part of the window and your code **('ViewController.swift')** on the right part of the window. See Figure 3-26 for reference.

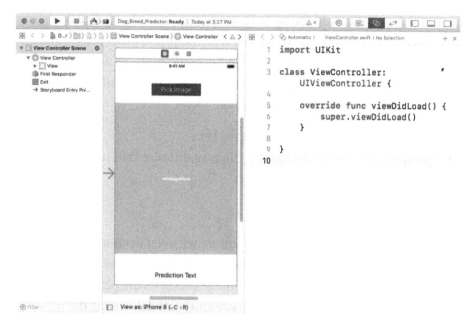

Figure 3-26. *Assistant editor*

Step 8: To connect interface elements to the code, we need to create outlets and actions. Create an outlet for Button, ImageView, and Label. Also create an action for the button. To do so, control and drag from the Button/Image View/Label to the code ("ViewController.swift"). If you are successful in creating outlets and actions for the UI elements, the following code will be added to your ViewController class:

```
@IBOutlet weak var predictionText: UILabel!
@IBOutlet weak var imageView: UIImageView!
@IBOutlet weak var btn: UIButton!

@IBAction func btnClick(_ sender: Any) {
}
```

Step 9: Now let us add the code that will handle the button click. First, since we need the user to interact with the photo library, we must conform to the UIImagePickerControllerDelegate protocol as well as UINavigationControllerDelegate protocol. Add both the controllers to you class definition in the ViewControllor.swift file:

```
class ViewController: UIViewController,
UIImagePickerControllerDelegate, UINavigationControllerDelegate {

    //code
}
```

Step 10: When the user clicks the button, we need to create an instance of UIImagePickerController and set its delegate to our current class. We also need to specify the source for the image picker as the photo library. Once the picker is created, we need to present it modally using the present method. To do so, add the following code to the pickImageBtnClick method in the ViewControllor.swift file:

```
@IBAction func btnClick(_ sender: Any) {

    let imagePicker = UIImagePickerController()

    imagePicker.delegate = self
    imagePicker.allowsEditing = false
    imagePicker.sourceType = .photoLibrary

    present(imagePicker, animated: true, completion: nil)
}
```

Step 11: Since we are confirming to the delegate for the image picker, we need to implement two delegate methods: imagePickerController and imagePickerControllerDidCancel. The imagePickerController method is called when the user is finished selecting the image from the library. Hence, we will use this method to set the selected image in the Image View of our application. The imagePickerControllerDidCancel method is called when the user cancels the image picker. Hence, in this method, we will simply dismiss the picker. Add the following code to the ViewController class in the ViewControllor.swift file:

```
func imagePickerController(_ picker: UIImagePickerController,
didFinishPickingMediaWithInfo info: [UIImagePickerController.
InfoKey : Any]) {

    let pickedImage = info[.originalImage]  as! UIImage

    imageView.image = pickedImage

    self.dismiss(animated: true, completion: nil)
}

func imagePickerControllerDidCancel(_ picker:
UIImagePickerController) {

    self.dismiss(animated: true, completion: nil)

}
```

Step 12: Since our application needs to access the photo library of the user's device, we need to ask the user to grant access for the same. Otherwise our application might terminate unexpectedly. To avoid that, we need to add the following property in the **"Info.plist"** file (Figure 3-27) of our application:

Key: Privacy – Photo Library Usage Description

Value: $(PRODUCT_NAME) photo use

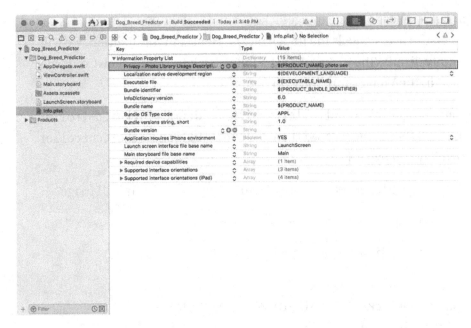

Figure 3-27. *Information property list*

Step 13: Now that we have created the application interface, let us add our custom model to the project. To do so, drag and drop the model file under your project folder in the Xcode project navigator. This will add the Core ML model in your application.

Step 14: Select the model file from the navigator and you will notice that the Xcode automatically recognizes the file as an ML model. It displays information about the model such as type of the model (which in our case is Neural Network Classifier), the size of the model, model description, and so on. See Figure 3-28 for reference.

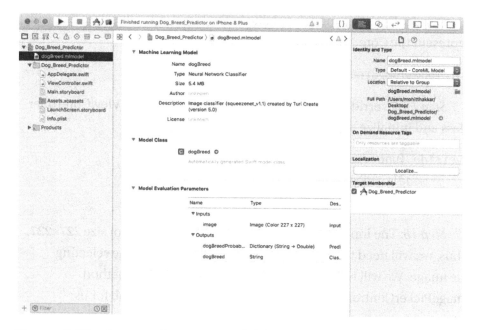

Figure 3-28. *Custom Core ML model (Dog_Breed_Predictor)*

It also displays the Model Class, which is automatically generated from the ML model and can be directly used in our application. Click the arrow next to the class name and you will be able to see the implementation code of the model class.

Other important information that the Xcode displays is the Model Evaluation Parameters. This is the information about the input that the model takes in and the output that it returns. In our case, the model takes in a colored image of size 227×227 as an input and it returns a string as output.

Step 15: Now let us use the model class in our application in order to make predictions. Go to the ViewController.swift file and import the Core ML framework in the very beginning.

```
import CoreML
```

Step 16: Declare a model variable in the ViewController class that will represent the Core ML model.

```
var model:dogBreed!
```

Step 17: Override the viewWillAppear() method of the ViewController class and initialize the model in that method.

```
override func viewWillAppear(_ animated: Bool) {
    model = dogBreed()
}
```

Step 18: The input that our model takes in is an image of size 227×227. Thus, we will need to resize the image after the user is done selecting the image. We will write the code for this in the delegate method imagePickerController(). The following code will do the job for us:

Note   The numbering in the following lines of code is just added for the explanation that follows, and the numbers are not a part of the code.

```
//resize image
```

1. `UIGraphicsBeginImageContextWithOptions (CGSize(width: 277, height: 277), true, 2.0)`
2. `pickedImage.draw(in: CGRect(x: 0, y: 0, width: 277, height: 277))`
3. `let newImage = UIGraphicsGetImageFromCurrentImageContext()!`
4. `UIGraphicsEndImageContext()`

5. `let attrs = [kCVPixelBufferCGImageCompatibilityKey: kCFBooleanTrue, kCVPixelBufferCGBitmapContextCompatibilityKey: kCFBooleanTrue] as CFDictionary`
6. `var pixelBuffer : CVPixelBuffer?`

```
7.  let status = CVPixelBufferCreate(kCFAllocatorDefault,
    Int(newImage.size.width), Int(newImage.size.height),
    kCVPixelFormatType_32ARGB, attrs, &pixelBuffer)

8.  guard (status == kCVReturnSuccess) else {
9.      return
10. }

11. CVPixelBufferLockBaseAddress(pixelBuffer!, CVPixelBufferLo
    ckFlags(rawValue: 0))

12. let pixelData = CVPixelBufferGetBaseAddress(pixelBuffer!)

13. let rgbColorSpace = CGColorSpaceCreateDeviceRGB()
14. let context = CGContext(data: pixelData, width:
    Int(newImage.size.width), height: Int(newImage.size.
    height), bitsPerComponent: 8, bytesPerRow: CVPixelBuff
    erGetBytesPerRow(pixelBuffer!), space: rgbColorSpace,
    bitmapInfo: CGImageAlphaInfo.noneSkipFirst.rawValue)

15. context?.translateBy(x: 0, y: newImage.size.height)
16. context?.scaleBy(x: 1.0, y: -1.0)

17. UIGraphicsPushContext(context!)
18. newImage.draw(in: CGRect(x: 0, y: 0, width: newImage.size.
    width, height: newImage.size.height))
19. UIGraphicsPopContext()
20. CVPixelBufferUnlockBaseAddress(pixelBuffer!, CVPixelBuffer
    LockFlags(rawValue: 0))
```

Now, let us understand what is happening in the preceding code. Since our model accepts an input image of size 227×227, lines 1-4 convert the selected image to that size and assign it to a new variable called newImage.

It is important to know that the model accepts an input image in the form of pixels. Hence, lines 5-10 store the newImage in the form of a pixel buffer, which basically holds the image in the form of pixels in the memory. This buffer will be supplied as an input for prediction.

Then, all the pixels present in the image are converted in to device dependent RGB color space. Lines 11-13 do that. In line 14, we store the pixel data in CGContext so that we can easily modify some properties of the image pixels. We then scale the image as per our requirement in lines 15-16. Lines 17-20 update the final image buffer.

Note that it's okay if you do not understand most parts of this code. The only thing you need to know is that we took the picture that the user selected from the photo library and converted it into a form that the model accepts for prediction.

Step 19: Finally, it's time to call the prediction method of the model that will do the image prediction for us. Add the following code in the delegate method imagePickerController() right after the image resizing code.

```
//predict image label

guard let prediction = try? model.prediction(image:
pixelBuffer!) else {
    predictionText.text = "Can't Predict!"
    return
}

predictionText.text = "Dog Breed:  \(prediction.dogBreed)."
```

The prediction method is supplied with the pixel buffer as a parameter. If the prediction is successful, the method returns an object that gives us the output label. We set this output label text to the classifier label that we added to the interface earlier. If the prediction is not successful, we manually set the classifier label text to let the user know that the model was unable to predict the label for the selected image.

Step 20: It is finally time to build and run the application. Let us find out how well our first ML application does. Figures 3-29 to Figure 3-33 show different screens that you should see while playing around with your application.

Figure 3-29. *Dog breed prediction (A)*

Figure 3-30. *Dog breed prediction (B)*

Figure 3-31. *Dog breed prediction (C)*

Figure 3-32. *Dog breed prediction (D)*

Figure 3-33. *Dog breed prediction (E)*

Summary

- There is no single model that can be used to perform all the intelligent tasks. Hence, we need different custom models for different tasks.

- The custom machine learning model can be created in five simple steps:

    - Define the problem

- Collect data

- Train the learning algorithm

- Evaluate the learning algorithm

- Build the model

- Apple introduced a Python-based package called Turi Create that helps us in creating custom ML models directly from the dataset.

- Turi Create uses a technique called transfer learning, that is, we can train our model on top of an already existing model. The learning of the existing model is transferred to our model; therefore we only need to train the last few layers of our model. This significantly reduces the training time as well as the size of our model.

- Apple also introduced Core ML Tools, which is a Python package that can be used to convert models from various formats to the Core ML format using very few lines of code.

- Once you convert an ML model to the Core ML format, it can be easily used in your application, just like any of the Apple-provided models.

CHAPTER 4

Custom Core ML Models Using Create ML

In Chapter 3, you learned how to train custom machine learning models using a third-party framework called Turi Create. This chapter introduces you to the Create ML framework introduced by Apple Inc. in 2018 to allow developers to train custom ML models for iOS applications. In addition to the image classification model that you trained in Chapter 3, this chapter introduces two more types of models: one trained using text-based data and the other trained using tabular data.

Introduction to Create ML

While Core ML takes care of integrating an ML model in your application, Create ML is used to build those ML models. Though it is possible to create custom ML models using Core ML Tools (just like we learned in Chapter 3), Apple introduced Create ML in 2018 to make things even simpler. Create ML is Apple's very own ML framework. The idea is to build your custom ML model using Create ML and then use it in your application using Core ML.

© Mohit Thakkar 2019
M. Thakkar, *Beginning Machine Learning in iOS*,
https://doi.org/10.1007/978-1-4842-4297-1_4

Rather than training your model in some other language and then using Swift to integrate it with your iOS application, Create ML allows a programmer to implement end-to-end ML in Swift. Moreover, you can use Create ML directly in your Xcode Playgrounds. Following are the types of data that can be trained into a model using Create ML. Figure 4-1 shows them as well.

- *Images*: This kind of data can be used to train a custom image classifier model that can recognize an object in the images.

- *Text*: This kind of data can be used to train a custom text classifier model that can be used to perform tasks like sentiment analysis, topic analysis, and domain analysis.

- *Tabular data*: This kind of data can be used to train a custom regression model that can be used to perform predictions of multiple kinds.

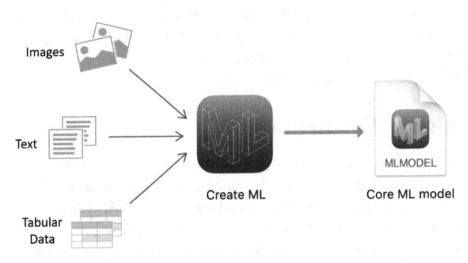

Figure 4-1. Data types trained into a model using Create ML

The workflow of a custom model creation using Create ML is same as the life cycle of custom model creation that we learned in Chapter 3. The steps include: problem identification, data gathering, training the model, evaluating the model, and generating the model. For more details, kindly refer to the relevant topics in Chapter 3.

In the following sections of this chapter, we will learn how to create an image classification model, text classification model, as well as a regression model using Create ML.

Image Classification

Image classification is a problem of determining what label you would like to apply to a given image. We will try to solve the same problem that we solved in the previous chapter, that is, dog breed identification, but this time using Create ML. The following is our problem statement:

Problem   *Given a picture of a dog, the model should be able to identify the breed of the dog.*

Now, you might already have the dataset that you created in Chapter 3. We will use the same dataset for this example. If you do not have the dataset, here is what you need to do:

- First, create a folder called Dataset on your MacBook.

- Inside the Dataset folder, create subfolders for each breed of dog you want to classify.

- Then inside each subfolder, place some images of dogs of that breed.

- Note that the name of the subfolder should be the breed of the dogs whose images that folder contains. Figure 4-2 shows the folder structure for the dataset.

Figure 4-2. Dataset for image classifier

That's it; you now have your dataset. The next step is to train your model using this data. Note that Create ML uses the same transfer learning technique that we learned about in Chapter 3 while learning about Turi Create. It means, using Create ML, we can train our model on top of an ML model that already exists in the OS. This results in faster training and smaller model size. Following are the steps to train an image classifier model using Create ML:

Step 1: Open Xcode; select **File ➤ New ➤ Playground** in the menu (Figure 4-3).

Figure 4-3. *New Playground in Xcode*

Step 2: Select the Blank file from the template selection menu (Figure 4-4). Note that you need to select a blank file under MacOS and not iOS, because the Create ML framework isn't supported for iOS Playgrounds.

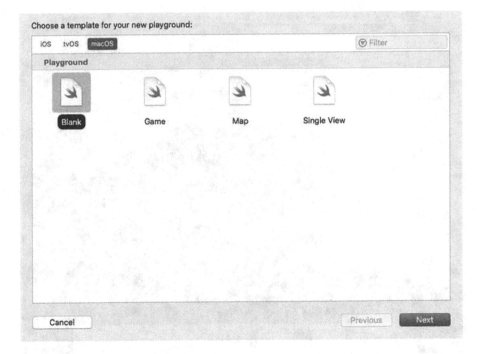

Figure 4-4. *Playground template selection*

Step 3: Name it **"DogBreedPredictor"** and save it to desktop.

Step 4: Now import Create MLUI by adding the following code to the Playground:

```
import CreateMLUI
```

Create MLUI is a framework similar to Create ML; the only difference is that unlike Create ML, it has a UI to it.

Step 5: Next, we will create a builder that will help us in training our model. To do so, add the following code:

```
let builder = MLImageClassifierBuilder()
```

Step 6: To work with the builder using the Live Demo feature of Create MLUI, we will use the following method in our code:

```
builder.showInLiveView()
```

Enable the Live Demo feature of Xcode by switching on the assistant editor from the toolbar. You will see a play button on the last line of your code. See Figure 4-5 for reference. Click that button to view the builder interface in the Live Demo.

Figure 4-5. *Live demo in Xcode Playground*

Step 7: You will notice that we need to drop images into the builder UI to begin training. This is quite simple. Select the Dataset folder, and drop the entire folder into the builder UI. As soon as you do this, the Playground will start training the model. The console at the bottom will show you the number of images processed, elapsed time, and the percentage of job done. See Figure 4-6 for reference.

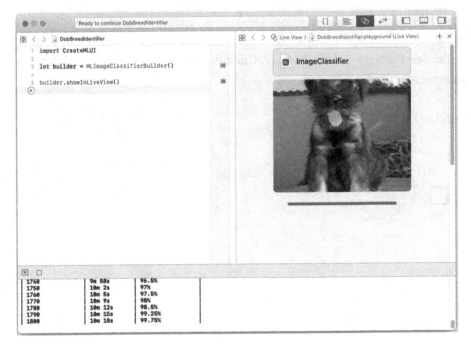

Figure 4-6. *Training image classifier using Create ML (A)*

When the training is done, the builder UI will show you three labels: Training, Validation, and Evaluation. See Figure 4-7 for reference.

- The training displays the amount of data Playground was successfully able to train. This should be 100%.

- Before training, Xcode puts aside some images from the training dataset, which it later uses for evaluating the model once it's trained. Validation displays the result of such evaluation.

- Evaluation should be blank because we are not explicitly testing the model on any data.

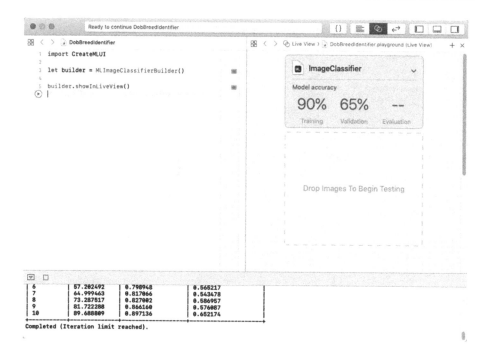

Figure 4-7. *Training image classifier using Create ML (B)*

Step 8: Let us see how good our model performs in determining the breed from unseen dog images. To do so, create a folder containing some unseen dog images (keep the folder structure the same as the training dataset) and drop it into the builder UI. The Playground will start testing the model. See Figure 4-8 for reference.

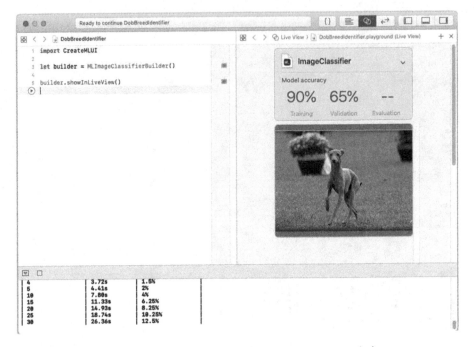

Figure 4-8. Testing image classifier using Create ML (A)

When testing is done, you will see a value for the Evaluation label. 100% means that the model classified all the images correctly. See Figure 4-9 for reference.

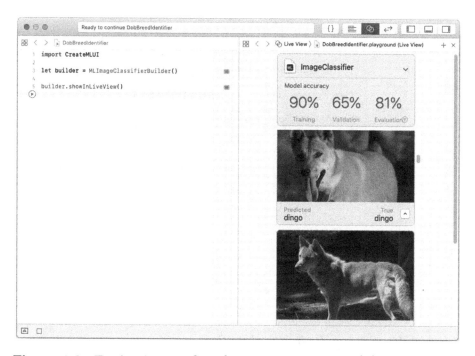

Figure 4-9. *Testing image classifier using Create ML (B)*

Step 9: If you are satisfied with the results, the next thing to do is to save the model. To do so, click the arrow next to the Image Classifier title in the Live Demo. A drop-down menu will appear, displaying all the metadata about the model, as shown in Figure 4-10. Change the metadata as per your preference and click Save.

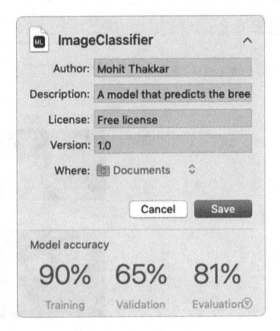

Figure 4-10. *Saving the image classifier*

That's how we build an ML Model using Create ML UI. If you do not want to use the builder UI and want to do this programmatically, following are the steps to do so:

Step 1: Open Xcode; select File ➤ New ➤ Playground in the menu.

Step 2: Select the Blank file from the template selection menu. Note that you need to select a blank file under MacOS and not iOS, because the Create ML framework isn't supported for iOS Playgrounds.

Step 3: Name it **"DogBreedPredictor"** and save it to desktop.

Step 4: Now import Create ML and Foundation by adding the following code to the Playground:

```
import CreateML
import Foundation
```

Step 5: Define the location of training dataset and test dataset by adding the following code:

```
let trainingLoc = URL(fileURLWithPath: "/Users/yourusername/
Desktop/MyDataset" )

let testLoc = URL(fileURLWithPath: "/Users/yourusername/
Desktop/MyTestData")
```

Step 6: Define the model by adding the following code:

```
let model = try MLImageClassifier(trainingData:
.labledDirectories(at: trainingLoc))
```

To begin training, press Shift+Enter. The console at the bottom will show you the number of images processed, elapsed time, and the percentage of job done. See Figure 4-11 for reference.

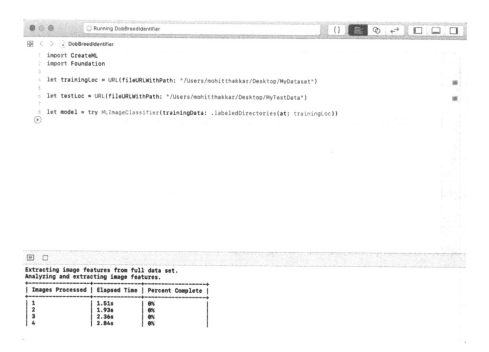

Figure 4-11. *Training image classifier using Create ML (C)*

Step 7: Now that training is done, you might want to evaluate the model based on the test data. To do so, add the following code:

```
let evaluation = model.evaluation(on:
.labledDirectories(at: testLoc))
```

To begin testing, press Shift+Enter. The console at the bottom will show you the evaluation output. See Figure 4-12 for reference.

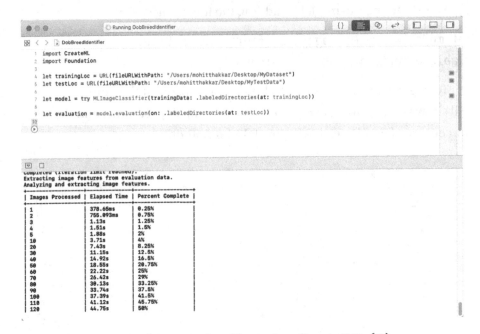

Figure 4-12.   *Testing image classifier using Create ML (C)*

Step 8: If you are happy with the evaluation results, it is time to save the model. To do so, add the following code:

```
try model.write(to: URL(fileURLWithPath: "/Users/yourusername/
Desktop/DogBreedPredictor"))
```

Press Shift+Enter and the model will be saved at the path you provided. Your final code should be as shown in Figure 4-13.

```
1  import Foundation
2  import CreateML
3
4  let trainingLoc = URL(fileURLWithPath: "/Users/mohitthakkar/Desktop/MyDataset")
5  let testLoc = URL(fileURLWithPath: "/Users/mohitthakkar/Desktop/MyTestData")
6
7  let model = try MLImageClassifier(trainingData: .labeledDirectories(at:
       trainingLoc))
8
9  let evaluation = model.evaluation(on: .labeledDirectories(at: testLoc))
10
11 try model.write(to: URL(fileURLWithPath: "/Users/yourusername/Desktop/
       DogBreedPredictor"))
```

Figure 4-13. *Image classifier using Create ML*

That's it. We just created an image classifier using Create ML that can predict the breed of a dog, given its picture. You can import this model into your iOS application and see how it performs.

Text Classification

Now that you know how to work with images, you might want to implement some ML tasks based on textual data (natural language). Such tasks include sentiment analysis, spam filtering, topic analysis, and so on. These tasks are commonly known as text classification tasks and the ML model that performs these tasks is known as a text classifier. Here, we will learn how to create an ML model that can perform sentiment analysis by classifying a piece of text.

To do so, we will first need some data on the basis of which we can train our model. Such data can be provided in the following forms:

- *Raw text files*: You can create labeled directories just like you did for the image classifier example. Each of these labeled directories will contain raw text files containing text that justifies the label. Consider the example in Figure 4-14.

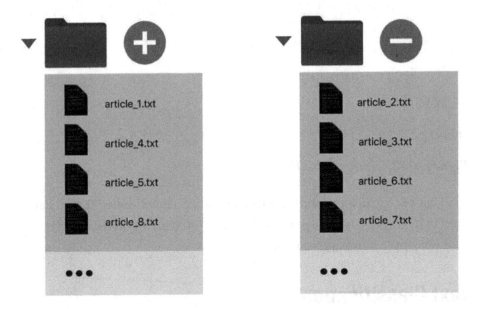

Figure 4-14. *Textual data for training*

Here, we have two labeled directories: one for positive data and one for negative data. The one with the "plus" label contains raw text articles containing positive texts, while the one with the "minus" label contains raw text articles containing negative texts.

- *CSV file*: Another way to organize your training data is to create a CSV (comma-separated values) file. Here, instead of separate files, all the data will be contained in one single file. Consider the example in Figure 4-15.

```
Japan is a great place to visit, POSITIVE
I hate going to the gym, NEGATIVE
Pizza is an awesome food item, POSITIVE
The world is a depressing place, NEGATIVE
```

Figure 4-15. *CSV data for training*

Here, we have a single file that contains entries for raw text and their respective truth label separated by a comma. This file can be used independently to train our ML model.

- *JSON file*: JSON stands for JavaScript Object Notation. It is an alternative data format to CSV. Just like a CSV file, a JSON file also contains all the data in one single file. It contains Key–Value pairs for representing the labeled data. Consider the example in Figure 4-16 to get a clearer idea.

```
{
        Text:       Japan is a great place to visit,
        Label:      POSITIVE
},
{

        Text:       I hate going to the gym,
        Label:      NEGATIVE
},
{

        Text:       Pizza is an awesome food item,
        Label:      POSITIVE
},
{

        Text:       The world is a depressing place,
        Label:      NEGATIVE
}
```

Figure 4-16. *JSON data for training*

Here, we have two keys for each piece of data: "Text"
representing the data and "Label'" representing the
truth label for the corresponding data. This file can
also be used independently to train our ML model.

Now that we are aware of the types of data that we can use to train a
text classification model, let us learn about the typical steps involved in the
training process. Following are the typical workflow steps for training a text
classifier (they are also shown in Figure 4-17):

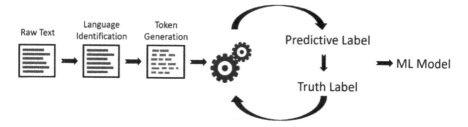

Figure 4-17. *Typical workflow for training a text classifier*

- *Raw data*: First, we collect the raw data that will be used for the training.

- *Language identification*: Then we identify the language from the raw text.

- *Token Generation*: Then we need to generate tokens from the text, which will be mapped against some labels by the learning algorithm.

- *Apply learning algorithm*: The learning algorithm will take the tokens as input and do some processing on them.

- *Get predictive label*: The learning algorithm will then give us the predicted label for the input tokens.

- *Compare it with truth label*: We will now compare the predicted label with the actual label for the raw text.

- *Reiterate*: If the prediction is not accurate enough, we will reiterate the training process.

- *Model generation*: If the prediction is accurate enough, we will generate the model.

However, using Create ML, all the complexities involved in the process can be reduced to very few, simple steps. Let us learn how to create, using Create ML, a text classifier that returns "Positive" if the input text is optimistic and returns "Negative" if the input text is pessimistic. To do so, we will first collect and organize our data.

Step 1: Create two folders: **"MyDataset"** and **"MyTestDataset"** on your Macbook.

Step 2: Create two subfolders: **"Positive"** and **"Negative"** for each of the two folders created in the previous step.

Step 3: Inside the folders named **"Positive,"** put some text files that contain sample positive comments. Inside folders named **"Negative,"** put some text files that contain sample negative comments. Refer to Figure 4-18 for the folder structure.

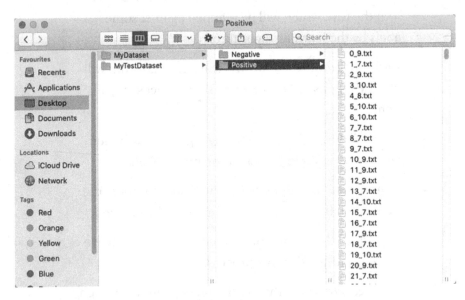

Figure 4-18. *Dataset for text classifier*

That's it. We now have the dataset required to train our model to perform the text classification task. Let us now train the model using the assembled data.

Step 1: Open Xcode; select **File ➤ New ➤ Playground** in the menu (Figure 4-19).

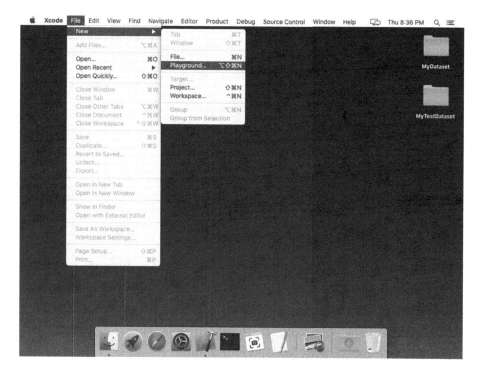

Figure 4-19. *New Playground in Xcode*

Step 2: Select the Blank file from the template selection menu (Figure 4-20). Note that you need to select a blank file under MacOS and not iOS because Create ML framework isn't supported for iOS Playgrounds.

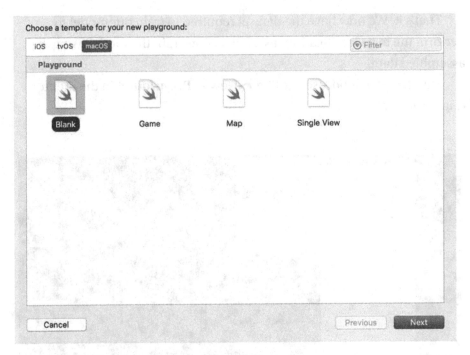

Figure 4-20. Playground template selection

Step 3: Name it **"SentimentAnalyzer"** and save it to desktop.

Step 4: Note that as of now, Create MLUI is only available for an Image Classifier and not for any other type of ML Model. So, we will have to use Create ML instead of Create MLUI. Add the following code to the Playground to import Create ML and Foundation:

```
import CreateML
import Foundation
```

Step 5: Define the location of the training dataset and test dataset by adding the following code:

```
let trainingLoc = URL(fileURLWithPath: "/Users/yourusername/
Desktop/MyDataset" )

let testLoc = URL(fileURLWithPath: "/Users/yourusername/
Desktop/MyTestDataset")
```

Step 6: Define the model by adding the following code:

```
let model = try MLTextClassifier(trainingData:
.labledDirectories(at: trainingLoc))
```

To begin training, press Shift+Enter. The console at the bottom will show you the number of training iterations and the accuracy for each iteration. See Figure 4-21 for reference.

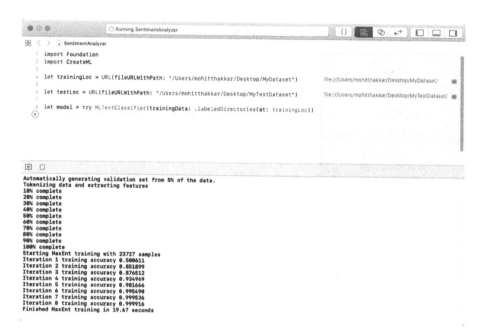

Figure 4-21. *Training text classifier using Create ML*

Step 7: Now that training is done, you might want to evaluate the model based on the test data. To do so, add the following code:

```
let evaluation = model.evaluation(on: .labledDirectories(at:
testLoc))
```

To begin testing, press Shift+Enter.

Step 8: Once the evaluation is done, it is time to save the model. To do so, add the following code:

```
try model.write(to: URL(fileURLWithPath: "/Users/yourusername/
Desktop/SentimentAnalyzer.mlmodel"))
```

Press Shift+Enter and the model will be saved at the path you provided. Your final code should be as in Figure 4-22.

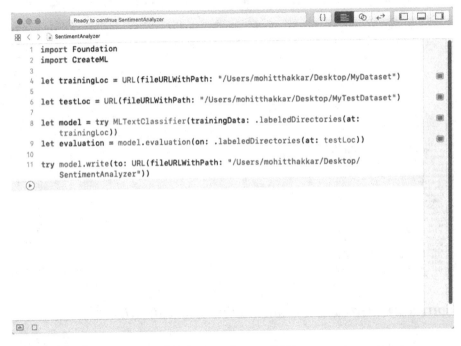

Figure 4-22. *Text classifier using Create ML*

If you have successfully executed the code, you will find an ML model named **"SentimentAnalyzer"** on your desktop (Figure 4-23).

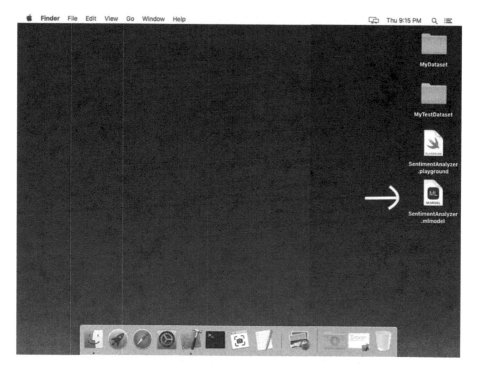

Figure 4-23. *Sentiment analysis model*

That's it. We just created a text classifier using Create ML that can predict the sentiment of the user on the basis of textual input. Let us now create an application to test this model. We will create an application that will allow the user to enter some text and, on the basis of the text entered, we will predict the emotional state of the user. If it is positive, we will enable the button that can be used to post the text on some social website. If it is negative, we will disable the button so that the user won't be able to post the negative content on the website.

Step 1: Open Xcode and create an iOS application project by following the steps that you've learned previously in this book.

Step 2: Open the **"Main.storyboard"** file to access the application interface. Add a Text View, a label, and a button. See Figure 4-24 for reference.

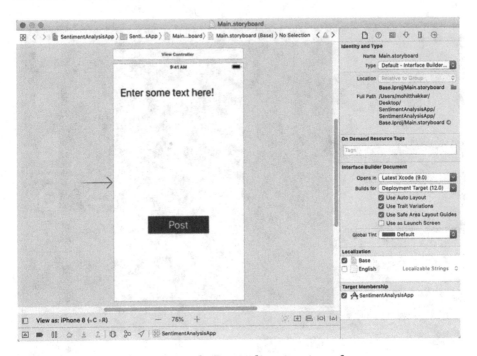

Figure 4-24. *Sentiment analysis application interface*

Step 3: Create necessary outlets for UI elements to help us access them in our code.

Step 4: Now, to capture the text change event of the text view, we will need our ViewController class to conform to the TextViewDelegate protocol. We also need to set the delegate for Text View in the viewDidLoad method. To do so, add the following code to the ViewController.swift file:

```swift
class ViewController: UIViewController, UITextViewDelegate {

    @IBOutlet weak var textView: UITextView!

    override func viewDidLoad() {

        super.viewDidLoad()
        textView.delegate = self;

    }

}
```

Step 5: Now to perform some action when the text in the textView is changed, we need to implement the textViewDidChange method of UITextViewDelegate protocol. To do so, add the following code to the ViewController class:

```
func textViewDidChange(_ textView: UITextView){
}
```

Step 6: It is now time to add our ML model to the app. Drag-and-drop the model file into your project folder in the navigation pane of Xcode. On selecting the model file, you will see various information such as Name, Type, Size, Author, and Description of the model. You can see the Swift code for the model by clicking the model name under the Model Class section. Under Model Evaluation Parameters, you will also see that the model takes in a string as input text and returns a string as an output label. Before using this model in our app, make sure that the target membership in the right pane is checked for your project. See Figure 4-25 for reference.

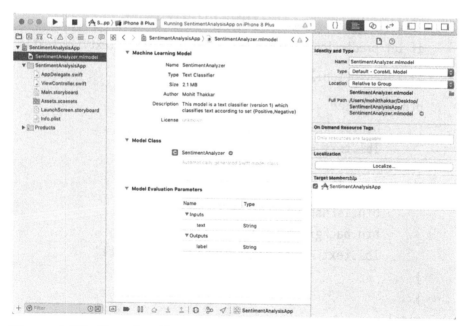

Figure 4-25. *Text classifier in Xcode*

Step 7: Now to use the model in our code, we will need to import the Core ML framework and declare a model variable in the ViewController class, which will represent the model. To do so, add the following code to the ViewController.swift file:

```
import CoreML
...
class ViewController: UIViewController, UITextViewDelegate {

    ...
    let model = SentimentAnalyzer()

    ...
}
...
```

Step 8: Now, to analyze the user sentiment we will call the prediction method every time the text in the TextView is changed. To do so, add the following code to the ViewController class:

```
func textViewDidChange(_ textView: UITextView) {

    if let prediction = try? model.prediction(text: textView.text){

    if (prediction.label.contains("Positive")){

    btn.isEnabled = true
        btn.backgroundColor = UIColor.green
        lbl.text = "Good to go!"
    }
    else{
        btn.isEnabled = false
        btn.backgroundColor = UIColor.red
        lbl.text = "Please Enter Positive Text!"
    }
    }
    else{
        btn.isEnabled = true
```

```
        btn.backgroundColor = UIColor.blue
        lbl.text = "Neutral Sentiment!"
    }
}
```

Step 9: It is finally time to build and run the application. Let us find out how well our ML model predicts the sentiment of the user. Figures 4-26 to Figure 4-28 show different screens that you should see while playing around with the application.

Figure 4-26. *Sentiment analysis application (A)*

Figure 4-27. *Sentiment analysis application (B)*

Figure 4-28. *Sentiment analysis application (C)*

Regression Model

Now that you know how to work with images as well as text, you might want to implement some ML tasks based on tabular data. Such data is normally used when you want to do some prediction based on multiple parameters. For instance, it can be used to predict the price for a house based on parameters such as neighborhood, total area of the house, number of bedrooms and baths, type of garage, number of levels the house has, and so on. Let us learn how to do this task using Create ML.

First of all, we will need the training data in tabular format. I have collected some tabular data that gives me the prices for houses in various neighborhoods in the United States. Figure 4-29 shows what the data looks like.

Area	Neighborhood	HouseStyle	FullBath	HalfBath	Bedroom	Kitchen	GarageType	SalePrice
8450	CollgCr	2Story	2	1	3	1	Attchd	208500
9600	Veenker	1Story	2	0	3	1	Attchd	181500
11250	CollgCr	2Story	2	1	3	1	Attchd	223500
9550	Crawfor	2Story	1	0	3	1	Detchd	140000
14260	NoRidge	2Story	2	1	4	1	Attchd	250000
14115	Mitchel	1.5Fin	1	1	1	1	Attchd	143000
10084	Somerst	1Story	2	0	3	1	Attchd	307000
10382	NWAmes	2Story	2	1	3	1	Attchd	200000
6120	OldTown	1.5Fin	2	0	2	2	Detchd	129900
7420	BrkSide	1.5Unf	1	0	2	2	Attchd	118000
11200	Sawyer	1Story	1	0	3	1	Detchd	129500
11924	NridgHt	2Story	3	0	4	1	BuiltIn	345000
12968	Sawyer	1Story	1	0	2	1	Detchd	144000
10652	CollgCr	1Story	2	0	3	1	Attchd	279500
10920	NAmes	1Story	1	1	2	1	Attchd	157000

Figure 4-29. *Tabular data for regression*

As you can see, the data describes houses in various neighborhoods along with their sale price. We will train our model on this data to predict the price of a house given the parameters. You can select a different dataset based on your preference and requirements. Let us go through the steps to train a regression model.

Step 1: Create a folder called **"Dataset"** on your Macbook.

Step 2: Store the tabular training data in a CSV file called **"train.csv."** Figure 4-30 shows the folder structure.

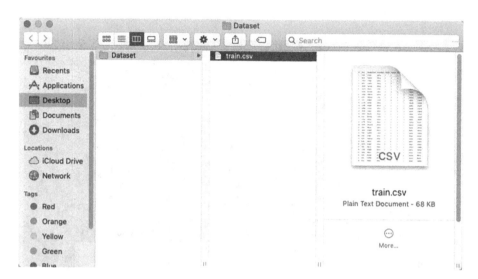

Figure 4-30. *Dataset for regression model*

Step 3: Open Xcode; select **File ➤ New ➤ Playground** in the menu (Figure 4-31).

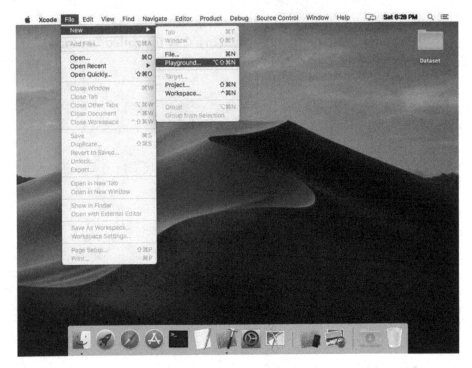

Figure 4-31. *New Playground in Xcode*

Step 4: Select the Blank file from the template selection menu (Figure 4-32). Note that you need to select a blank file under MacOS and not iOS because Create ML framework isn't supported for iOS Playgrounds.

Figure 4-32. *Playground template selection*

Step 5: Name it **"HousePricePredictor"** and save it to desktop.

Step 6: Note that as of now, Create MLUI is only available for an Image Classifier and not for any other type of ML Model. So, we will have to use Create ML instead of Create MLUI. Add the following code to the Playground to import Create ML and Foundation:

```
import CreateML
import Foundation
```

Step 7: Define the location of the training dataset by adding the following code:

```
let trainingLoc = URL(fileURLWithPath: "/Users/yourusername/
Desktop/Dataset/train.csv"     )
```

Step 8: Note that Create ML contains a special data structure called MLDataTable that makes it easy to deal with tabular data. We will have to create MLDataTables for our training data. To do so, add the following code to the Playground:

```
let houseData = try MLDataTable(contentsOf: trainingLoc)
```

Step 9: Split some test data from the training data so that we can test the model once it is trained. To do so, add the following code:

```
let (trainingData, testData) = houseData.randomSplit(by:0.8, seed: 0)
```

Step 10: Define the model by adding the following code:

```
let model = try MLRegressor(trainingData: trainingData,
targetColumn: "SalePrice")
```

To begin training, press Shift+Enter. The console at the bottom will show you the data for each iteration of training. See Figure 4-33 for reference.

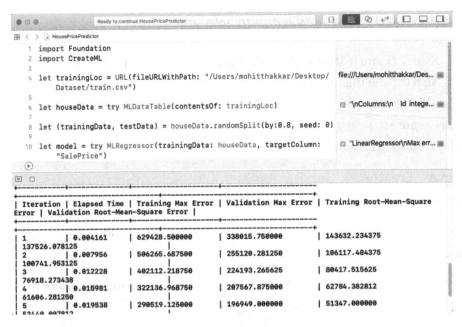

Figure 4-33. *Training regression model using Create ML*

Step 11: Now that training is done, you might want to evaluate the model based on the test data. To do so, add the following code:

```
let evaluation =      model.testingMetrics(on:testData)
```

To begin testing, press Shift+Enter.

Step 12: Once the evaluation is done, it is time to add some metadata and save the model. To do so, add the following code:

```
let modeldata = MLModelMetadata(author: "Mohit Thakkar",
shortDescription: "Model that      predicts house prices",
license: "Open Source",      version: "1.0")

try model.write(to: URL(fileURLWithPath: "/Users/mohitthakkar/
Desktop/HousePricePredictor.mlmodel"), metadata: modeldata)
```

Press Shift+Enter and the model will be saved at the path you provided. Your final code should be as shown in Figure 4-34.

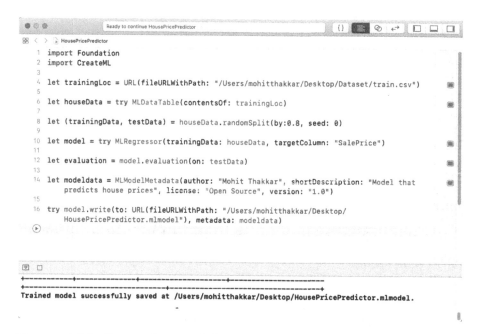

Figure 4-34. *Regression model using Create ML*

That's it. Our model is now ready to predict house prices. If you open the MLModel file (Figure 4-35), you will notice that the model takes in various house parameters such as neighborhood, total area of the house, number of bedrooms and baths, type of garage, and number of levels the house has, and it returns the house price as an output.

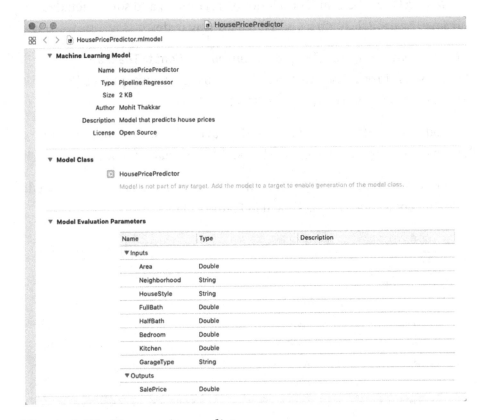

Figure 4-35. *House price predictor*

Now that we have created the regression model, let us create an iOS application to see if the model really works. We will create an application that allows users to enter the details about their dream house. And on the click of a button, we will fetch those details and use our model to predict the price. We will then display the house price to the user on the application interface.

Step 1: Open Xcode and create an iOS application project by following the steps that you've learned previously in this book. You can use the interface shown in Figure 4-36 as a reference.

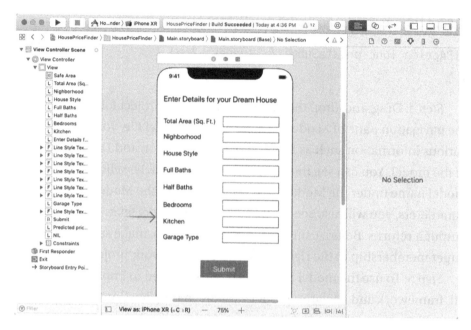

Figure 4-36. *House price finder application interface*

Step 2: Open the **"Main.storyboard"** file to access the application interface.

Step 3: Create outlets for the fields that describe the house and also for the label that will display the predicted price for the house. Also create an action for the button click event. This will add the following code to your ViewController class:

```
@IBOutlet weak var area: UITextField!
@IBOutlet weak var neighborhood: UITextField!
@IBOutlet weak var houseStyle: UITextField!
@IBOutlet weak var fullBaths: UITextField!
```

133

```
@IBOutlet weak var halfBaths: UITextField!
@IBOutlet weak var bedrooms: UITextField!
@IBOutlet weak var kitchen: UITextField!
@IBOutlet weak var garageType: UITextField!
@IBOutlet weak var housePrice: UILabel!

@IBAction func onDataSubmit(_ sender: Any) {
}
```

Step 4: Drag-and-drop the model file into your project folder in the navigation pane of Xcode. On selecting the model file, you will see various information such as Name, Type, Size, Author, and Description of the model. You can see the Swift code for the model by clicking the model name under the Model Class section. Under the Model Evaluation Parameters, you will also see the inputs that the model takes in and the output it returns. Before using this model in our app, make sure that the target membership in the right pane is checked for your project.

Step 5: To use the model in our code, we will need to import the Core ML framework and declare a model variable in the ViewController class that will represent the model. To do so, add the following code to your ViewController.swift file:

```
import CoreML
...
class ViewController: UIViewController {
    ...
    let model = SentimentAnalyzer()
    ...
}
...
```

Step 6: Now to predict the house price, we will call the prediction method when the submit button is tapped. We will also set the value of the label to the predicted price that the model returns. To do so, add the following code to the ViewController class:

```
@IBAction func onDataSubmit(_ sender: Any) {

let prediction = try? model.prediction(Area: Double(area.text!) ?? 0,
Neighborhood: neighborhood.text!,
HouseStyle: houseStyle.text!,
FullBath: Double(fullBaths.text!) ?? 0,
HalfBath: Double(halfBaths.text!) ?? 0,
Bedroom: Double(bedrooms.text!) ?? 0,
Kitchen: Double(kitchen.text!) ?? 0,
GarageType: garageType.text!)

    housePrice.text = "\(String(describing: prediction!.SalePrice))"
}
```

Step 7: It is finally time to build and run the application. Let us find out how well our ML model predicts the house price for the user's dream house. Figures 4-37 and 4-38 show different screens that you should see while playing around with your application.

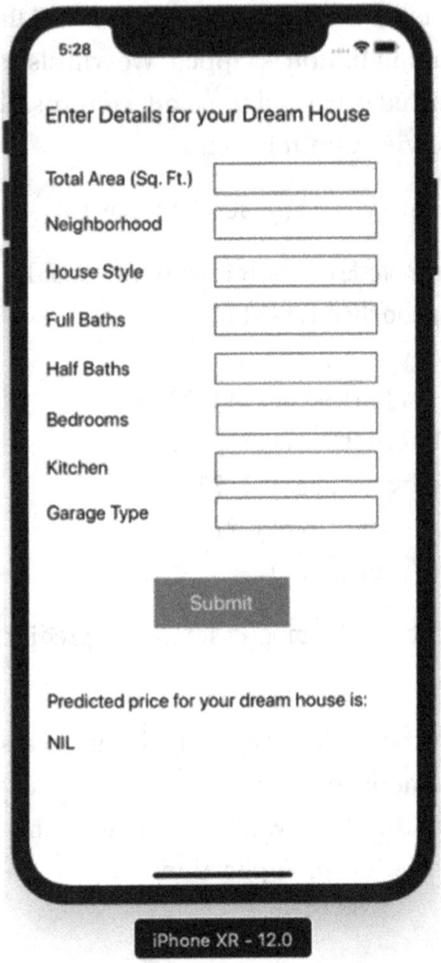

Figure 4-37. *House price finder application (A)*

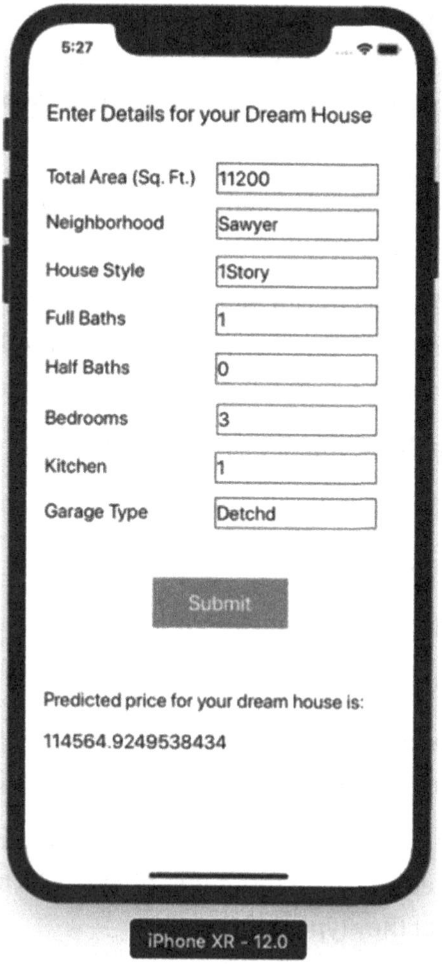

Figure 4-38. *House price finder application (B)*

Summary

- Apple introduced Create ML in 2018 to provide developers with the capability to implement end-to-end machine learning in Swift.

- Though ML models can be created using previously launched Core ML tools, Create ML does the job even easier with its direct integration with Xcode Playgrounds.

- Major types of data that can be trained into a model using Create ML are images, text, and tabular data.

- The workflow of custom model creation using Create ML is the same as the life cycle of custom model creation that we learned in Chapter 3. It is as follows:

  - Define the problem

  - Collect data

  - Train the learning algorithm

  - Evaluate the Learning Algorithm

  - Build the model

- Image classifier models can be built to accomplish tasks such as prediction of dog breed from its image.

- Text classifier models can be built to accomplish tasks such as predicting the sentiment of the users based on the text that they type.

- Regression models can be built to accomplish tasks such as predicting the price of a house based on its locality, net area, type of house, and multiple other factors.

CHAPTER 5

Improving Computational Efficiency

This chapter shares with the reader's information on some miscellaneous topics such as the difference between GPU and CPU processing, and things to consider while implementing machine learning.

More importantly, this chapter covers two important frameworks that the Core ML framework is based on: Accelerate and Metal Performance Shaders (MPS). There are no practical examples of using these two frameworks in code because they are implicitly used while implementing ML using Core ML. However, the chapter covers abstract information on the libraries that these two frameworks comprise.

GPU vs. CPU Processing

The CPU (Central Processing Unit) is often called the brain of a machine. The majority of the software on the machine requires a CPU to function. However, there are several examples of software that requires heavy computation power. A CPU cannot efficiently support the functioning of such software. This is where a GPU (graphics processing unit) comes to the rescue.

© Mohit Thakkar 2019
M. Thakkar, *Beginning Machine Learning in iOS*,
https://doi.org/10.1007/978-1-4842-4297-1_5

A GPU is a special kind of microprocessor that is designed for quick image rendering. GPUs were launched as a solution to graphically potent applications that consumes a lot of CPU power and degrades the overall machine performance. However, modern GPUs are even capable of handling applications that require powerful mathematical calculations. With the use of GPUs, whenever software needs heavy computation power, the process is transferred from CPU to GPU to preserve the overall performance quality of the machine. Figure 5-1 shows the abstract structure of CPUs and GPUs.

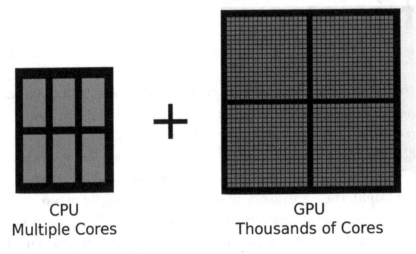

CPU
Multiple Cores

GPU
Thousands of Cores

Figure 5-1. *CPU vs. GPU*

Though a CPU and GPU are both silicon-based microprocessors, they process tasks in very different ways. While a CPU is referred to as the brain of a machine, a GPU is referred to as the muscle of the machine. A CPU is good at performing multiple, diverse kinds of tasks but it can run only few tasks at a time due to its limited number of cores. Whereas a GPU focuses all its computation power in carrying out one specific kind of task, but it can run multiple instances of similar tasks due to its large number of cores. A CPU has up to 24 cores, which are designed to optimize the performance of a single task within a job. On the other hand, a GPU has thousands of smaller cores, which are optimized for handling multiple tasks in a parallel architecture. Modern GPUs are used to address tasks such as ML and big data analysis.

Key Considerations while Implementing Machine Learning

While implementing ML on a mobile device, we tend to lose some of the luxuries that we get while implementing it on a computer. Following are some of the points to consider while implementing ML in a mobile application:

- *Model size*: In previous chapters we walked through the process of building some simple ML models, which are negligible in terms of memory requirements. But, as you dive into the world of ML, it's common to find models hundreds of megabytes in size. For example, the VGG16 model is a 16-layer neural network architecture trained on the ImageNet dataset used for image classification. It is available on Apple's site and is approximately 500 megabytes in size. Asking your user to download such a large file may intimidate them.

- *Memory*: Along with the overall size of the model, you also need to be concerned about the amount of working memory that the model might require. It is not uncommon for desktop computers to have around 16 to 32 Gigabytes of memory, but the latest iPhone (iPhone XS Max) has merely 4 Gigabytes of RAM. This constraint should be kept in mind while selecting the ML model for your mobile application.

- *Processing speed*: This is a factor that depends on multiple things. Loading the input data and making the inference is not the only part of the workflow. There is certain preprocessing as well as postprocessing associated with the functioning of the application. For instance, if the input text is in string format and your model only accepts an array input, you might want to convert the string into an array before making the inference. This is referred to as preprocessing. In the same way, if the model returns a string label as an output but you want to display an emoticon to the user, you might want to map the string to the corresponding emoticon before displaying it to the user. This is referred to as postprocessing. At times, you might have to trade off some processing speed against large model size.

Accelerate

Accelerate is a framework that was first introduced by Apple in 2003 for Mac OS X v10.3 Panther. It is a collection of high-performance vector-accelerated libraries that lets you perform vector-based operations in your application without explicitly using low-level vector instructions. You do not need to be concerned with the user's machine because the Accelerate framework is written to automatically invoke the appropriate instruction set based on the architecture of the machine that the code is running on. Figure 5-2 shows the libraries that the Accelerate framework is comprised of.

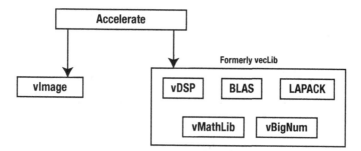

Figure 5-2. *Accelerate framework in Panther*

vImage – Image Transformation

The vImage library contains routines to perform operations on graphics and images. These routines make the best use of available hardware. They can perform operations such as the following:

- *Format conversion*: The vImage library primarily supports image formats such as Planar8, PlanarF, ARGB8888, and ARGBFFFF. It supports image conversion between these formats.

- *Convolution*: This is a term that refers to the process of modifying pixel values based on the values of the pixels surrounding it. Convolution can be used to implement image effects such as blur, sharpening, embossing, and so on. The vImage library also supports deconvolution, which is a process of reversing the effect of convolution.

- *Morphological operations*: These are the operations that are used to modify the structure of an image. The vImage library supports two morphological operations: dilation, where the size of the pixels is gradually increased; and erosion, where the size of the pixels is gradually decreased.

- *Histograms*: The histogram for an image is used to graphically describe the intensities of the image pixels. The vImage library supports the creation of image histograms. Moreover, one can also transform an image to have the same pixel intensities as a particular histogram.

- *Geometric operations*: The vImage library provides subroutines that can geometrically transform images. The operations include Rotate, Flip, Warp, Mirror, Scale, and so on.

- *Alpha compositing*: Each pixel in an image has an alpha value that determines the opaqueness of the pixel. Alpha compositing is the process of merging two images with different alpha values and producing an image that would give the effect as if one image is placed on top of another.

- *Transformation operations*: The vImage library also supports pixel transformation functions that do not depend upon the value of other pixels. The functions include matrix multiplication and gamma correction.

vDSP – Digital Signal Processing

The vDSP library is primarily focused on Fourier transforms, matrix arithmetic, and vector operations. The applications of the vDSP library includes speech processing, audio processing, digital image processing, cryptography, and other vector operations such as finding the absolute value of a vector, converting between a single precision vector and a double precision vector, compressing vector values, and so on. vDSP subroutines operate on basic C data types such as float, integer, double, short integer, and character.

BLAS and LAPACK

The Basic Linear Algebra Subprograms (BLAS) and Linear Algebra Package (LAPACK) libraries contain subroutines to perform matrix-based linear algebra computations such as eigenvalue problems and matrix multiplication. BLAS acts as a base library for LAPACK that performs advanced algebraic computations.

vMathLib

The vMathLib is a vector-centric version of the standard math library libm. The difference between them is that vMathLib uses 128-bit hardware vectors to perform mathematical operations.

vBigNum

The vBigNum library performs operations such as integer addition, substraction, division, and multiplication using 1024-bit integer operands.

To use the Accelerate libraries in your Xcode project, you will need to add the Accelerate header file in your project by adding the following code:

```
#include <Accelerate/Accelerate.h>
OR
import Accelerate
```

You will also need to add the framework to your project from the system frameworks folder:

```
.../System/Library/Frameworks/Accelerate.framework
```

Note   Accelerate is a complex framework and is not a recommended way to begin machine learning in iOS. As a beginner, all you need to know is that Core ML, the latest framework for ML, is based on Accelerate and harnesses the computational capabilities of the Accelerate framework.

Metal Performance Shaders

MPS is a framework that was announced by Apple at WWDC 2015. It is a collection of optimized, high-performance image processing algorithms for iOS 9. MPS uses the device GPU for compute-heavy tasks. The functions in the MPS framework implement most of the common image processing tasks such as blur, convolution, histogram, resampling, and so on. These functions act as a black box to developers. The major benefit of this is that Apple can modify and improve the framework as per the availability of better hardware, while the developers do not need to worry about the framework code. Figure 5-3 shows the class hierarchy for the MPS framework.

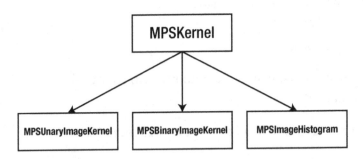

Figure 5-3.   *MPS framework architecture*

All the classes in the MPS framework are derived from a class called MPSKernel. A kernel in this context refers to a set of weights that are combined with the source image to produce an output image. MPSKernel, as a class, does nothing but create a copy of the kernel and gives it a name. The real job is done by the three subclasses of MPSKernel: MPSUnaryImageKernel, MPSBinaryImageKernel, and MPSImageHistogram.

A unary image kernel takes in a single texture as an input and produces a single output texture. There are several categories of unary operation that can be performed using MPSUnaryImageKernel. Every operation has its own class that inherits from MPSUnaryImageKernel. The naming convention for these subclasses is in a fashion such that the operation name is prefixed by MPSImage. For instance, if the operation to be performed is Gaussian Blur, the class name will be MPSImageGaussianBlur. Following are the operations supported by MPSUnaryImageKernel:

- *Convolutional operations*: Box, Tent, GaussianBlur (Figure 5-4), Sobel (Figure 5-6), Convolution (general)

- *Thresholding*: ThresholdBinary, ThresholdBinaryInverse, ThresholdToZero (Figure 5-5), ThresholdToZeroInverse, ThresholdTruncate

- *Lanczos resampling*: LanczosScale (down-scale, up-scale, squeeze, stretch)

- *Morphological operations*: erode, dilute, min, max

- *Sliding neighborhood operations*: Integral, IntegralOfSquares, AreaMax, AreaMin, Median, Threshold

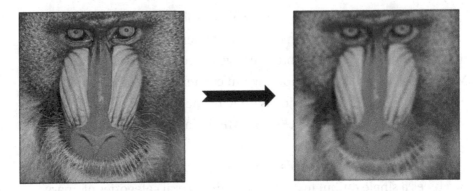

Figure 5-4. *Gaussian blur using MPS*

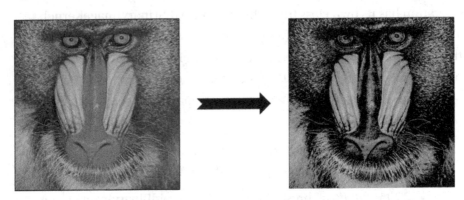

Figure 5-5. *Threshold to zero using MPS*

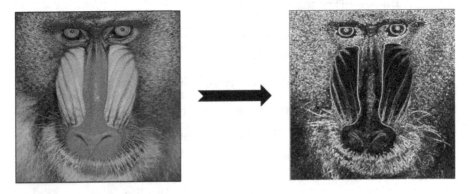

Figure 5-6. *Sobel edge detection using MPS*

A binary image kernel, unlike unary image kernels, takes in two textures as an input to produce a single output texture. Although there is a class called MPSBinaryImageKernel dedicated for the processing of binary images, there are no concrete subclasses inheriting from this class. Hence, we can only assume that this class is for developers to inherit from and write some custom code for the binary image operations that they want to perform.

MPSImageHistogram is a class that is used to compute the histogram of an image. Just like UnaryImageKernel, MPSImageHistogram also works on single-input texture. Typically, the histogram of the image is subsequently passed on to the MPSImageHistogramEqualization or MPSImageHistogramSpecification. The equalization filter allows equalization of the color intensities in your image to a uniform set of values (Figure 5-7), whereas the specification filter is used to modify your image histogram to match a histogram that you can specify.

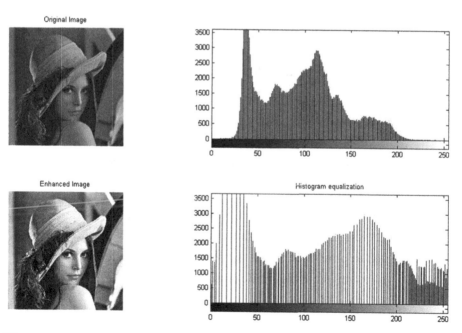

Figure 5-7. *Histogram equalization using MPS*

As an ML beginner, all you need to know is that when you create an image classifier model using Create ML, or perform inference using Core ML, the MPS framework plays a vital role in the underlying processes.

Summary

- A Central Processing Unit (CPU) is used for lightweight applications that do not require much computational power, whereas a Graphics Processing Unit (GPU) is used for applications that are graphically or mathematically potent and might degrades the overall machine performance if processed using a CPU.

- Model size, memory, and processing speed are three important factors to consider while implementing ML in mobile applications.

- The size for an ML model may be as big as 500 megabytes. It is a good practice to choose the model based on the computational power of the target machine.

- While selecting the ML model for your application, you also need to keep in mind that the working memory for computer devices might range from 16 to 32 gigabytes but the same for a mobile device might be limited to just 4 megabytes.

- Accelerate is a framework that was released by Apple in 2003 to provide libraries for vector computations, signal processing, and algebraic computations.

- The Accelerate framework comprises libraries such as vImage, vDSP, BLAS, LAPACK, vMathLib, and vBigNum.

- Metal Performance Shaders (MPS) is a framework that was released by Apple in 2015. It is a collection of optimized, high-performance image processing algorithms for iOS 9 that uses the device GPU for compute-heavy tasks.

- MPS provides classes for image processing tasks such as convolution, thresholding, resampling, morphological operations, histogram generation, equalization, and so on.

- Apple's latest ML framework, Core ML, is based on both Accelerate and MPS.

Index

© Mohit Thakkar 2019
M. Thakkar, *Beginning Machine Learning in iOS*,
https://doi.org/10.1007/978-1-4842-4297-1

Printed in the United States
By Bookmasters